D1073843

A PLAY MAKER OF NORTH CAROLINA

Harold Williamson as JED in his own play, *Peggy*, a tragedy of the tenant farmer.

FIRST SERIES

CAROLINA FOLK-PLAYS

Edited
With an Introduction on FOLK-PLAY MAKING
By

FREDERICK H. KOCH
Founder and Director of The Carolina Playmakers

Illustrated from photographs of the original productions of the plays

NEW YORK
HENRY HOLT AND COMPANY

All of these plays have been successfully produced.

A royalty fee is required for each performance of any of these plays, either by amateurs or by professionals. Special arrangements must be made for radio-broadcasting.

No performance of these plays may be given without full acknowledgment to The Carolina Playmakers, Inc., and to the publishers. Acknowledgment should be made to read as follows: "From the *Carolina Folk-Plays* edited by FREDERICK H. KOCH, Director. Produced by arrangements with The Carolina Playmakers, Inc., and with the publishers."

The amateur acting rights to these plays are controlled by Samuel French, 25 West 45th St., New York, N. Y., to whom application should be made for production.

The plays in this volume can be read or played anywhere, upon payment of the royalty required. While it would be well for the actors to study the hints on pronunciation in the Appendix of this volume still, outside of the Carolinas, the parts can be effectively played by actors speaking more or less in the manner of the country folk in whatever state the play is being presented.

Printed in the
United States of America

TO
"THE ONLIE BEGETTER"
E. G.

THE PLAYMAKERS' AIM

FIRST: *To encourage and promote dramatic art, especially by the production and publishing of plays.*

SECOND: *To serve as an experimental theatre for the young playwright seeking to translate into fresh dramatic forms the traditions and present-day life of the people.*

THIRD: *To extend their influence in the establishment of a native theatre in other states.*

CONTENTS

ILLUSTRATIONS

FOLK-PLAY MAKING

By Frederick H. Koch

Founder of The Dakota Playmakers and The Carolina Playmakers

The *Carolina Folk-Plays* suggest the beginnings of a new native theatre. They are pioneer plays of North Carolina life. The stories and characters are drawn by the writers from their own tradition, and from their observation of the lives of their own people.

They are wholly native—simple plays of the locality, of common experience and of common interest. North Carolina is rich in legends and in historical incident; she is rich too in the variety and virility of her present-day life. There is in these plays something of the tang of the Carolina soil. There is something of the isolation of her mountains and their sheltering coves; something of the sun and the wind of the farm lands; of the shadowy thickets of Scuffletown Swamp; something, too, of the loneliness of the lives of the fisher-folk on the shifting banks of Nags Head or Cape Lookout.

They were written by sons and daughters of Carolina, at Chapel Hill, the seat of the state university. They have been produced with enthusiasm and success by The Carolina Playmakers in their own town and in many towns all over the state. The Carolina Playmakers is a group of amateurs—*amateurs* in the original and full sense of the word—devoted to the establishment of a theatre of coöperative folk-arts. Not a single cloth has been painted by an outsider. Everything has been designed and made in the home town in a truly communal way.

To be sure they are plays of a single section, of a single state, North Carolina. But they have a wider significance. We know that if we speak for the human nature in our own neighborhood we shall be expressing for all. The locality, if it be truly interpreted, is the only universal. It has been so in all lasting literature. And in every locality all over America, as here in North Carolina to-day, there is the need and the striving for a fresh expression of our common folk life.

THE BEGINNINGS IN NORTH DAKOTA

The North Carolina plays represent the cumulation of years of experiment. The beginnings at the University of North Dakota, located at Grand Forks, were simple enough. It is now sixteen years since the writer made the first "barn-storming" tour, in 1906, over the treeless levels of Dakota with a company of University players. The play was Richard Brinsley Sheridan's admirable comedy, *The Rivals,* to be followed in succeeding tours with such old favorites as Goldsmith's *She Stoops to Conquer,* Dickens' *Tom Pinch,* and Sheridan Knowles' *The Love Chase.* In this way the ground was cleared and made ready for a people's drama of sound foundations.

A remarkable development of dramatic interest followed, and an enthusiastic fellowship of players was formed. It grew, and became in good time a flourishing society of play-makers—The Dakota Playmakers—pledged to the production of native plays of their prairie country.

Two different types of drama developed naturally—the pageant, a distinctly communal form enlisting actively all the people; and the folk-play, an intimate portrayal of the life and character of the people of the plains.

DAKOTA COMMUNAL DRAMA

In the Dakota pageantry a new form of creative literary work was evolved—communal authorship. The historical *Pageant of the North-West* in 1914, and the tercentenary masque, *Shakespeare, The Playmaker,* in 1916, were designed and written entirely—dialogue, poetry, and music—by a group of these amateur Playmakers in collaboration, eighteen in the first case and twenty in the second. And the published play-books proved that the people themselves, when rightly directed, could create their own dramatic forms, in phrases "filled with liveliness and humor, and with no little imagination" in a coöperative native drama "never amateurish and sometimes reaching a high literary level." [1]

Such production required a theatre in the open. There was no hill-slope and, by the necessity of the prairie land, a new type of native theatre was discovered. So the Bankside Theatre came to be "the first open-air theatre to make use of the natural curve of a stream to separate the stage from the amphitheatre,"[1] and a contribution was made of permanent value in the history of the out-door stage.

In succeeding years of this renaissance—for such indeed it proved to be—The Dakota Playmakers carried out over the state their new-found means of dramatic expression, directing the country people in many parts of North Dakota in the writing and staging of pageants and plays of their own local traditions.

DAKOTA FOLK-PLAYS

At the same time The Playmakers at the university were busy writing for their improvised "Play-Stage" a variety of simple folk-plays portraying scenes of ranch and farm life, adventures of the frontier settlers, incidents of the cowboy trails.

Then they toured the state with their new-made Prairie Plays using a simple portable stage of their own devising. And the people in the towns visited received them with wonder and enthusiasm. They knew them for their own, and were honestly proud and happy about it. Everybody said, "Come again, and we'll give

---

[1] "Dakotan Discoveries in Dual Dramaturgy," by Hiram K. Moderwell, in *The Boston Evening Tronscript,* September 30, 1916.

you a bigger audience next time!" The little folk-play had found its own.

Typical of these prairie plays perhaps is *Barley Beards* by Howard DeLong, who was born of French homesteaders in a sod shanty forty miles from the railroad. *Barley Beards* deals with an I. W. W. riot in a North Dakota threshing crew and is based on young DeLong's experiences on a Dakota wheat farm at harvest time. The author himself designed and painted the scenery, and acted a leading part in his play.

Other one-act pieces of this type are: *Back on the Old Farm* by Arthur Cloetingh, suggesting the futility of the "high-brow" education when it goes back to the country home at Long Prairie; *Dakota Dick,* by Harold Wylie, a comedy of the Bad Lands of the frontier days; and *Me an' Bill,* by Ben Sherman of Judith Basin, Montana, a tragedy of the "loony" sheep-herder, well-known to the playwright, and his love of the lonely shepherd's life on the great plains:

"You are out there on the plains, under the blue sky, with the soft winds a-singin' songs to you. Free—God, but you're free! You get up in the morning to meet the sun; you throw out your arms, breathe into your lungs life; and it makes you live—it makes you live! It is the same feelin' He had. He wanted to live for his sheep. (*Then addressing his spectral dog he chuckles to himself.*) Did you catch him, Shep?"

Full of the poetry of the North-West country are the words of Tim Nolan in the romance of the old Irish pioneer in *For the Colleen* by Agnes O'Connor:

"Hers was the face that 'u'd haunt the heart and the dreams of such a lonely Irish lad as Tim Nolan was, on the big prairie. And I began to work my claim as I'd never done before—dreamin' all the time of a little home. Just a wee house with a white picket fence around it—with wild roses growin' everywhere. Just Mary and me, and the green of the grass, and the spring winds blowin' fresh, and the meadow-lark singin'."

Such are the country folk-plays of Dakota—simple plays, sometimes crude, but always near to the good, strong, wind-swept soil. They tell of the long bitter winters in the little sod shanty. But they sing too of the springtime of unflecked sunshine, of the wilderness gay with wild roses, of the fenceless fields welling over with lark song! They are plays of the travail and the achievement of a pioneer people.

THE CAROLINA PLAYMAKERS

The work of The Dakota Playmakers was noted in various parts of the country. In North Carolina, Dr. Edwin Greenlaw, Head of the Department of English in the state university, saw a rich field for the making of a native folk drama. His insight and continuing loyalty have made possible the remarkable growth of the idea there.

North Carolina extends more than five hundred miles from the Great Smoky Mountains on the western border to the treacherous shoals of Hatteras. In the backlands of these mountains and among the dunes of the shifting coast line may be found "neighborhoods" where the customs of the first English settlers still prevail, where folk-tales still survive in words and phrase long since obsolete to us, handed down by word of mouth from one generation to another through all the years of their isolation.

And in North Carolina, too, we have the ballads and the lore of an outlived past side by side with the new life of the present day. Here are still the fine old families of the first Cavaliers and the children of the plantation days of the Old South. In contrast with these is the dreary "one-horse" farm of the poor white tenant and the shiftless negro. In greater contrast, perhaps, is the toil of the thousands of workers at the roaring mills.

North Carolina is still without large cities, and a strong folk-consciousness persists. The State is still regarded by the people as a family of "folks," due to the fact that the population is almost pure Anglo Saxon and still remarkably homogeneous. For all the changing industrial conditions less than two per cent of the inhabitants of the State are of foreign birth or parentage. Here the home talents are still cherished as a means of genuine enjoyment. The people have not broken their connections with the big family of the country folks. They have retained their birthright of pleasure in simple things. It is not strange that from such a spirit of neighborliness a native drama should spring.

A new fellowship of Playmakers came naturally in

the fall of 1918. There was no formal organization at first. Membership in The Carolina Playmakers was open to all. Anyone who did anything toward the making of a play was counted a Playmaker. It was truly a society of amateurs in coöperative folk-arts.

Already a wide range of original folk-plays have come. They were written in the University course in Dramatic Composition, and produced by The Playmakers on a home-made stage, constructed by them for the purpose, in the auditorium of the Public School building at Chapel Hill.

The initial program consisted of *What Will Barbara Say?* a romance of Chapel Hill by Minnie Shepherd Sparrow who essayed the leading part; *The Return of Buck Gavin,* a tragedy of a mountain outlaw, by Thomas C. Wolfe, of Asheville, who made his début as a player in the title rôle of this his first play; and *When Witches Ride,* a play of North Carolina folk-superstition drawn largely by the young author, Elizabeth A. Lay, from her own experiences while teaching in a country school in Northampton County.

The prologue, *Our Heritage,* written by Miss Lay for the occasion, expresses beautifully The Playmakers' faith:

> We mock with facts the Southern folk-belief,
> And so forget the eternal quest that strove
> With signs and tales to symbolize the awe
> Of powers in heaven and earth still undefined.
> Yet we may catch the child-like wondering
> Of our old negroes and the country folk,
> And live again in simple times of faith

And fear and wonder if we stage their life.
Then witches ride the stormy, thundering sky,
And signs and omens fill believing minds;
Then old traditions live in simple speech
And ours the heritage of wondering!

The production was entirely home-made; the scenery as well as the settings, costumes, and make-up all done in the little home town. Miss Lay tells how she scoured the countryside to find a log cabin to serve as a model for the scene in her initial play, *When Witches Ride,* how she "sketched the details and drew in the logs on the big canvases," and how after "weeks of experiment with the new kind of paint—weeks in which the scene resembled a layer cake or a striped flag more than anything else"—finally the medium was mastered and a really creditable log cabin set achieved.

The first performance of new plays is an event long to be remembered. There is a feeling of intimate interest, an almost childlike excitement on the part of everyone—townspeople, students and professors alike. This is *their play,* written by one of their own number. These are their players, and all are Playmakers together.

It is an interesting experience to participate with the audience in such a performance. "If the log cabin used in a play of fisher-people contains logs larger than the trees in that section," Miss Lay remarked one day, "if the rocks in the fireplace could not have existed, in that locality, if there is a flaw in the dialect, the author and producer will be sure to hear about it." For the audience is genuinely interested in the reality of the play and the stage picture must be true to the life, even in the least details.

The play is *Peggy,* perhaps. The curtain discloses the shabby interior of a tenant cabin. It is a familiar sight—just such a drab-looking cabin in the red fields as each person present has passed by many times without thought or interest. Mag, the jaded farm woman with snuff-stick protruding from the corner of her mouth, is getting supper, singing snatches of an old ballad as she works. She is a commonplace figure. But in the play she becomes a character of new and compelling interest. Spontaneous guffaws of laughter greet this actual appearance upon their stage of the "sorry-looking," snuff-spitting character so familiar to them. But presently all are moved to feel with the actors the tragic fact of her hard-won existence. Then, it seemed to me, that the dividing footlights were gone —that *the audience had actually joined with the actors and become a part of the play itself.* It had become a living truth to them.

The author, Harold Williamson, is playing the part of Jed, the stolid, good-hearted farmhand, with a homely sincerity and naturalness which recalls the work of the Irish Players. Sympathy, simplicity, the abandonment of self in the reality of the scene—these qualities in the acting serve to unite the people in the audience with the players on the stage. It is life itself before them "that moves and feels."

The plays produced in these first years have revealed a remarkable variety of materials and forms.

Representative of the farm plays are such tragedies of revolt as *Peggy, The Miser* and *The Lord's Will.* The second of these centres in the character of old Wash Lucas, "the stingiest man living in Harnett County," who hoards his wealth in a steel box and starves the lives of his children. After seeing this piece when it was presented in Raleigh on The Playmakers' State Tour last season, one remarked, "I know every member of that family. It is every bit true!" *The Lord's Will* has the same poignant reality. It tells the story of a country preacher, Lem Adams, the itinerant revivalist of the "tent-meetings," well known in the rural districts of North Carolina. It is the tragedy of a defeated dreamer. In contrast with these are *Dogwood Bushes* and *In Dixon's Kitchen,* comedies of the Carolina springtime, of the dogwoods and the peach trees all in bloom, and the old, old story of a country courtship.

There are plays of daring outlaws, the Croatan gang in *The Last of the Lowries* from the southern part of the State; and mountain plays of moonshiners and adventurers such as *Dod Gast Ye Both!, Reward Offered, The Return of Buck Gavin,* and the ghost-tale of *The Third Night.* There are colorful themes from Colonial times—the strange legend of *The Old Man of Edenton,* the wistful fantasy of *Trista,* the haunting mystery of Theodosia Burr in *Off Nags Head;* plays of the folk-belief in the supernatural as in *The Hag* and in the brave sea-play *Blackbeard, Pirate of the Carolina Coast,* with the gallant song of Bloody Ed, the buccaneer:

In a winding shroud of green seaweed
  There many a dead man lies—
And the waves above them glitter at night
  With the stare of the dead men's eyes.
No rest, no sleep, ten-fathom deep
  They watch with their glittering eyes.

Forever washed by the deep sea-tides
  With the changing coral sands,
For their treasured gold in their own deep graves
  They search with their bony hands.
No rest, no sleep, ten-fathom deep
  They dig with their bony hands.

There are also plays of North Carolina to-day—serious pieces like *Who Pays,* suggested by an incident which occurred during a strike in a southern city, and *The Reaping,* dealing with a social problem based on the Doctor's Report, side by side with the amusing sketches of college life like *The Vamp* and *The Chatham Rabbit* done in the picturesque phrase of our student vernacular; and *Waffles for Breakfast,* a happy satire of newly married life.

Not the least significant are the plays written for a negro theatre, such as the realistic *Granny Boling, The Fighting Corporal,* a rollicking comedy of the undoing of a braggart soldier just back from "de big war in France," and *White Dresses,* the story of Old Aunt Candace and her niece, Mary McLean, a pretty quadroon girl. Aunt Candace becomes the embodiment of her race, and her words to Mary conclude the stark tragedy of the race problem: "I knows yo'se got feelin's, chile. But yo'se got to smother' em in. Yo'se got to smother 'em in."

In preparing the texts of the plays the aim has been to preserve the naturalness of the speech. The spelling of the dialect has been simplified as much as possible without destroying the distinguishing local characteristics of the language as spoken in North Carolina. The Southern dialect is hard to represent in print. In the task of editing the dialect of the plays The Playmakers are indebted to the expert and devoted services of Professor Tom Peete Cross, formerly of the University of North Carolina, now of the University of Chicago. The results of his scholarly zeal in this difficult field are admirably summarized in his article on "The Language of the Plays" prepared for the appendix to this volume. It will serve as an invaluable guide to the player in the pronunciation of the vernacular as spoken in the South.

A brief statement of the sources of the plays included in this volume will suggest to the reader the nature and the variety of our Carolina materials.

WHEN WITCHES RIDE

The characters and the superstition in this play were drawn largely from the author's observation as a country school teacher in Northampton County, North

Carolina. The idea of the plot is based on the following account of the actual character, Phoebe Ward, given in an article by Professor Tom Peete Cross of the University of Chicago on "Folk-Lore from the Southern States," published in *The Journal of American Folk-Lore,* Volume XXII (1909).

"The early years of Phoebe Ward, witch, are shrouded in mystery. . . . She lived here and there, first at one place and then at another in Northampton County, North Carolina. She stayed in a hut or any shelter whatsoever that was granted her.

"She made her living begging from place to place. Most people were afraid to refuse her, lest she should apply her witchcraft to them. . . . Hence the people resorted to a number of methods to keep her away. For instance, when they saw her coming, they would stick pins point-up in the chair bottoms, and then offer her one of these chairs. It is said that she could always tell when the chair was thus fixed, and would never sit in it. Also they would throw red pepper into the fire, and Phoebe would leave as soon as she smelled it burning. . . .

"Among her arts it is said that she could ride persons at night (the same as nightmares), that she could ride horses at night, and that when the mane was tangled in the morning it was because the witch had made stirrups of the plaits. She was said to be able to go through key-holes. . . . She was credited with possessing a sort of grease which she could apply and then slip out of her skin and go out on her night rambles, and on her return get back again."

PEGGY

The characters in this play were drawn from life. "Although far from typical of North Carolina, such conditions as are here portrayed are not uncommon in some localities," the author writes. "The action of the play is a true transcript of the family life of the characters in the play, as I have known them in real life."

"DOD GAST YE BOTH!"

This is a play dealing with moonshiners of western North Carolina. It is a comedy of folk characters lifted out of contemporary life and portrayed through the medium of drama.

A group of mountaineers, lounging around a blockade still which nestled in a thicket of rhododendron and laurel on the side of Grandfather Mountain, one summer day not long ago decided to play a trick on old Noah Setzer, a moonshiner and boss of the Ridge, by telling him that his daughter Mary had "fell" for a certain suspicious stranger who had come into those parts and who was believed to be a "revenooer." Out of this prank and the results that came from it, the plot was developed.

After writing the play, the author took it back to the Hills and read it to Noah one winter evening by his still. To find himself in a play and to hear his very words spoken again quite amazed and delighted the old man. He laughed as he heard again how he had been fooled into getting a "revenooer" for a son-in-law. As he got up to stir his mash, he said, "But hit was a kind o' unnad'ral joke to pull on me atter all!"

Last summer on the occasion of another visit to the scene of his play, Mr. Heffner, the author, found old Sank, the boot-legger for old Noah (whose part he himself played in the original cast) in jail for moonshining.

OFF NAGS HEAD, or THE BELL BUOY

In the winter of 1812, according to the legend, a pilot boat drifted ashore at Kitty Hawk, near Nags Head, on the coast of North Carolina. In the cabin, among other evidences of the presence on the boat of a woman of wealth and refinement, was found a portrait of a lady. The "bankers," the rough, half barbarous inhabitants of the islands along the North Carolina coast, cut off from the moderating influences of mainland civilization, were in the habit of regarding all driftwood, regardless of its size or condition, as their own property. They fell upon deserted vessels and demolished them. This small pilot boat was treated in the customary manner. The portrait fell into the hands of a fisherman, on whose walls it hung for many years.

In 1869, Dr. William G. Pool was called in to see, near Nags Head, an old fisherwoman, who was sick. He found the portrait, secured possession of it and its story, and later identified the subject as Theodosia Burr, daughter of Aaron Burr.

In a small pilot boat, *The Patriot,* on December 30, 1812, Mrs. Theodosia Burr Alston sailed from Georgetown, South Carolina, for New York, where she expected to join her father who had just returned from exile. *The Patriot* did not reach New York; neither it nor any of its crew or passengers was ever heard of again. The commonly accepted story is that the boat was taken by pirates and the persons on board forced to walk the plank.

These are the two stories.

The "bankers" of the North Carolina coast are known, at this time, not to have confined their wrecking activities to the victims that chance threw in their way. They evolved a scheme by which vessels were lured upon the sandy beach by a light fastened to a horse's head, which from a distance looked like a ship at anchor, or moving slowly. When the deluded ship came aground, these land pirates boarded it and, killing the persons on board, plundered the vessel.

These things, told by Miss Pool in *The Eyrie,** and a suggestion made by her furnish the basis for *Off Nags Head.* Miss Pool says, "It is not improbable that *The Patriot* during a night of storm was lured ashore by a decoy light at Nags Head, and that passengers and crew fell into the hands of the land pirates in waiting, who possessed themselves of the boat and everything of value it contained.

---

* *The Eyrie and Other Southern Stories* by Bettie Freshwater Pool. New York. 1905.

THE LAST OF THE LOWRIES

This play is based on the account given by Mrs. Mary C. Norment in *The Lowrie History* (Daily Journal Print, Wilmington, N. C., 1875). Part of the action is not historical. In reality Steve Lowrie and not Henry Berry was the last of the gang.

The Lowries were a famous band of outlaws of mixed blood, part Croatan Indian. In the latter part of the Civil War many of the Croatans in Robeson County were opposed to the conscription of men by the Confederate Government for work on the fortifications along Cape Fear. Among these were the Lowrie boys, who killed an officer sent to arrest them for evading the law. After this, the Lowries concealed themselves in Scuffletown Swamp where they were supplied with food by their sympathizers. As the gang grew in size it began to act on the offensive instead of the defensive, and soon it spread terror throughout the county, robbing, plundering, and killing when necessary. For more than ten years the gang held out against the officers of the law and only in 1874 was the last Lowrie killed.

No particular effort is made to follow the intricacies of the Croatan dialect. But the following characteristics of pronunciation will be of aid in giving the play local color.

The typical Croatan of 1874 spoke with a peculiar drawl in his voice, most often pronouncing his *t* like *d,* as "better," *bedder; c* or *ck* was pronounced like *g,* as "back," *bag;* short *a* like short *o,* as "man," *mon.*

Sometimes *g* was sounded as *d,* as "loving," *lovind.* Even now there is little change in the dialect of the uneducated Croatans.

In the woodcut at the beginning of this article, designed by Mr. Julius J. Lankes as a program-heading for The Carolina Playmakers, a mountaineer on one side and a pirate on the other draw the curtains on a Carolina Folk-Play, *The Last of the Lowries,* suggesting the wide range of materials from which these plays are drawn.

Such are the *Carolina Folk-Plays.*

They have been welcomed in towns and cities all over North Carolina. It is the hope of our Playmakers that they will have something of real human interest for the big family of our American folk beyond the borders of Carolina.

There is everywhere an awakening of the folk-consciousness, which should be cherished in a new republic of active literature. As did the Greeks and our far-seeing Eliabethan forebears, so should we, the people of this new Renaissance, find fresh dramatic forms to express our America of to-day—our larger conception of the kingdom of humanity.

Toward this The Carolina Playmakers are hoping to contribute something of lasting value in the making of a new folk theatre and a new folk literature.

Chapel Hill, North Carolina.
September 30, 1922.

WHEN WITCHES RIDE[1]

A Play of Folk-Superstition

BY

ELIZABETH A. LAY

WHEN WITCHES RIDE

CAST OF CHARACTERS

As originally produced at The Play-House, Chapel Hill, North Carolina, March 14 and 15, 1919.

UNCLE BENNY, *owner of the crossroads store,*	George McF. McKie
ED, *his son,*	Walter H. Williamson
JAKE, *formerly a railroad engineer,*	George Denny
PHOEBE WARD, *witch*	Alga E. Leavitt

SCENE: The storehouse of a cross-roads store. The action takes place in the back country of North Carolina, near the Roanoke River, at a time when the people of Northampton County still believed in witches. A stormy night.

SCENE

THE storehouse of a cross-roads store.

The room is a typical log cabin, roughly built. Red peppers, herbs, and dried vegetables hang from the low rafters. Boxes and bales are piled in disorder among farm implements, kitchen utensils, and miscellaneous articles from the stock of a cross-roads general store. Dust and cobwebs are everywhere. In the back wall at the right a small opening cut in the logs serves as a window, with a rough shutter hinged loosely at the right side. The door in the back wall at the left is hidden by a dirty sheet, hung over it to keep out the cold air. In the right side-wall is a huge stone fireplace in which a hot fire blazes, the opening being nearly filled with logs. A large supply of wood is piled beside the fireplace at the right. A big jug of liquor stands on a box in that corner. There is a rough bench in front of the fire. In the front at the left is a table. Three lighted candles, a small straw-covered jug, mugs of liquor, and coins are on the table.

ED, JAKE, *and* UNCLE BENNY *are seated around the table, playing cards and drinking. Outside the storm is gathering.*

UNCLE BENNY *is very old. His face is wrinkled and weather-beaten. He has no teeth and is nearly bald. He wears an old shirt and rusty trousers.*

Ed is middle-aged, red of face, very tall and lank. His shoulders droop and his whole appearance is that of slouchiness. He wears a dirty shirt with sleeves rolled up, and ragged overalls.

Jake is older than Ed. He is burly and strong, commanding respect from the others who fear his bad temper. He is something of a bully. He wears a dark coat over his overalls. An old engineer's cap is on his head.

UNCLE BENNY

(*Speaking in a high, nervous voice*)

This here's mighty good liquor, ain't it so, Jake?

JAKE

(*Pours himself another glass*)

Uh-huh. (*Gruffly.*) It's your play, Ed.

UNCLE BENNY

I reckon you might's well pour me some more, too, while you're 'bout it.

(JAKE *pours while* UNCLE BENNY *holds his cup. Suddenly a loud crash of thunder is heard.* UNCLE BENNY *starts up and jerks his hand away, nearly spilling the contents of the jug.*)

JAKE

(*Grabs the jug and sets it down with a bang*)

Drat your hide, ol' man! Do you want to waste all this good whiskey? What's the matter with you? Hey?

UNCLE BENNY

Thar now, Jake, I didn't mean no harm.

JAKE

I reckon you nigh about wasted all this here liquor!

ED

(*Drawling, testily*)

Well, 'tain't none of your liquor, is it?

JAKE

(*Turning on him*)

An' what're you jumpin' in about? You're both 'bout to jump out'n your skins! What you feared of? 'Tain't nothin' but thunderin' a mite.

UNCLE BENNY

But it's an awful night, Jake. It's witch weather—thunder an' lightnin' on a cold night like this here—jest the night for witches to be ridin' an' sperits to be walkin' an' I can't leave off from feelin' that bad luck's a-comin' to us here. (*A very loud thunder clap is heard as the storm grows more fierce.*) Oh, lordy! lordy!

ED

Hit's one powerful queer storm, sure, but brace up, Pop, 'n have another drink.

(*The mugs are filled again*)

UNCLE BENNY

Mighty strange things has happened on a night like this here, an' right nigh the Roanoke River here, too.

I mind as how 'twas jest sech a storm as this when a ol' witch rid my ol' woman to death. Yes, suh, when she woke up in the mornin' they was dirt in between her fingers, an' her hair was all tangled up whar the witch had done made stirrups of it for to ride her through the briars. She was nigh about wore out, an' all she could do was to stare an' gape an' mumble 'bout goin' through the key-hole. . . .

JAKE

(*Scornfully*)

Aw, shucks! Your ol' woman drunk herself to death an' I reckon it didn't take much ridin' to finish her, neither. If you'd been drivin' a railroad engine nigh about all over Carolina an' into Virginia like I have, you'd 'a seen so many sights that it'd take more'n any ol' hag to give you the shakes. Any ol' back-country witch like Phoebe Ward can't scare me off from a good dram like this here, let me tell you all that!

ED

They do say ol' Phoebe herself is prowlin' round in this neighborhood, her'n that durned ol' toad she carries round. She slept 'cross the river last night an' Jeff Bailey seen her cuttin' through the low-grounds 'bout dawn.

JAKE

Wal, I'd jest like to see ol' witch Phoebe one more time an' I'd finish for her. 'Clare to goodness the last time she come roun' to my house I fixed her good an' purty. (*Laughing loudly.*) I chucked the fire right full of red pepper pods an' she nigh about sneezed her head off. It didn't take ol' Phoebe long to pick up that toad of hers an' clear out of there, damned if it did! I reckon she won't come soon again to stay with me!

UNCLE BENNY

(*Fearfully. Rolling thunder is heard*)

They do say as how she was married to the Devil hisself once. I've heared 'em say he's comin' hisself an' carry her off one of these days when her time's come.

JAKE

I reckon he'll get us all when our times comes, for all that. (*Laughing coarsely.*) Aw, brace up, Benny! I'd like to get my hands on that ol' toad.

(UNCLE BENNY *looks around fearfully, as though dreading her appearance. He gets up and shuffles slowly to the fireplace, speaking as he goes.*)

UNCLE BENNY

I've heared tell it was her toad that's her sperit. The varmint leads her to a place an' then sets on the hearth stones 'twell it's time for her to move. She won't stir from that place 'twell her ol' Gibbie commences to hop off first.

JAKE

She didn't wait for her toad to hop last time she visited me, let me tell you-all that!

UNCLE BENNY

You'd best to mind how you rile ol' Phoebe, Jake. They do say as him what angers her will be witched. They say her spell'll pass on him, an' Gibbie'll be his sperit. He'll have to move when that toad commences to hop jest the same as ol' Phoebe.

JAKE

Aw, I'd like to see any ol' toad-frog make me move on. A good jug of liquor's the only thing'd put a spell on me!

ED

(*Rises and speaks to* UNCLE BENNY *who is warming his hands at the fire*)

Let's have another dram, Pop.

(*As they stoop over the big jug in the corner to the right, a terrific thunder crash is heard. They drop the jug with a bang and* JAKE *strides over to them in a rage.*

The witch has entered unseen, having slipped through the curtain over the door. PHOEBE WARD *is very old, and bent, and wrinkled. Her dress is wrapped around her in rags and on her head she wears an old bonnet which does not hide her wizened face. There are two pockets in her skirt. She stands rubbing her hands, pinched and blue with the cold.*)

JAKE

(*With his back to the door. He has not seen* PHOEBE)

Damn you, give me that jug, you two ol' fools! Are

you goin' to waste all the liquor yet? (*The others are bending over the jug, paralyzed by the sight of* PHOEBE, *who advances slowly into the room.*) What're you starin' at? (*He wheels around, sees* PHOEBE, *and starts back in amazement.*) The witch!

(*There is a dead silence while* PHOEBE *shivers toward the fire.*)

ED

(*Hoarsely*)

Good Lord! How'd she get in?

UNCLE BENNY

(*Cowering in fear*)

Sure's you're born she's done come through the latch-hole!

JAKE

(*Hesitating*)

What you doin' here?

PHOEBE

(*She ignores* JAKE *and comes down centre.* ED *and* UNCLE BENNY *cross to the left as she advances, and retreat behind the table in fear. She speaks to an object concealed in her pocket.*)

Sh, now, Gibbie, quit your hoppin'. (*She takes the toad out of her pocket, shuffles slowly to the right and puts the toad on the end of the bench.*) Sh, now, this here's whar you'll leave me rest a bit now, ain't it? Thar now, toad-frog. (*She crosses to the right of the table.*) Uncle Benny, I'se powerful tired. I'se done come nigh onto ten mile from the river. Leave me rest a spell, me'n Gibbie?

UNCLE BENNY

Sure, now . . .

JAKE

(*Takes a step forward, menacingly*)

Get out of here, you damned witch!

(ED *and* UNCLE BENNY *regard his boldness with alarm.*)

PHOEBE

(*Slowly turns to* JAKE, *watching the effect of her words, which make even* JAKE *draw back.*)

Tain't no good luck it'll bring to you, Jake, if you drives me out again into the storm. My spell'll pass on him 'at harms me, an' the sperits'll be drivin' him like they drive ol' Phoebe. For it's my ol' man, the Devil, you'll be reckonin' with this time. It's the demons what're ridin' in the storm. Them an' Gibbie, they'll be drivin',—ain't it so, Gibbie? Drivin', drivin', an' never restin' 'twell Gibbie rests! Won't you leave me warm myself a bit, poor ol' Phoebe what the sperits has been drivin'?

ED

Don't rile her, Jake, don't rile her.

JAKE

(*Grudgingly, as he goes to the back of the room*)

Wal, set down, Phoebe, an' warm yourself—(*Turns*

on her)—but you got to ride yourself off presently, you hear me?

(*He comes down toward the table.* PHOEBE *sits down on the bench, looking very helpless and old.*)

PHOEBE

'Tain't as if I'll ever warm myself again, Jake. 'Tain't as if I'll ever set again an' watch the flames a-snappin' an' the sap a-sizzlin' in the hickory logs! When my Gibbie starts to hoppin' off from me this time, poor ol' Phoebe's 'bliged to go. She'll be gone for good, Jake, an' this here's the last time you'll lay your eyes on this poor ol' woman, Jake, this here's the last time . . . this here's the last time . . .

(*Mumbling.*)

JAKE

What're you talkin' about, Phoebe? Are you studyin' for to ride off home to hell with your Ol' Man, the Devil?

UNCLE BENNY

(*Hoarsely*)

She's goin' to ride us all to death, Jake. Don't make her witch us. Leave her be!

PHOEBE

(*A loud crash and roll of thunder is heard as the storm increases. The shutter and door rattle loudly in the wind.* PHOEBE *looks around wildly.*)

I done hyeard the Black Uns callin' in the thunder.

(*She rises and goes to the window.*) The Devil's ridin' on the fiery blaze o' lightnin' an' the Black Uns are a-screechin' in the wind. (*Frenzied.*) Oh, they're straddlin' on the storm clouds an' they're leanin' down an' stretchin' out an' callin' for ol' Phoebe. Don't you hear 'em, Jake, don't you hear them voices shriekin'? (*The wind blows loudly.*) Don't you hear them demon claws a-scratchin' at the door? They're callin' me, ain't they, Gibbie? An' when my time's done up, I'll go ridin' through the storm clouds an' this here's the last time you'll be seein' me on this earth. This here's the last time, ain't it, Gibbie?

(*She mumbles to herself.*)

ED

Aw, what's she mumblin' 'bout?

(*The candles flare in the draft.*)

UNCLE BENNY

Look! Look, Jake, we've got three candles a-burnin' an' it's a sure sign of death in this place. (*Quavering.*) Don't let her curse us all by dyin' in this place!

(*He goes to* JAKE *and seizes him appealingly.*)

JAKE

Aw, I ain't no witch doctor!

PHOEBE

Be you feared I'll leave this here ol' corpse behind me when I go? Oh, the Black Uns'll be callin' when my time's done over here an' the Devil hisself'll take me to be ridin' by his side. I'll be ridin' on the storm clouds as they thunders through the sky! I'll be ridin' off in lightnin' an' you won't see no trace o' Phoebe left behin'. . . . Jest a little while . . . jest a little while. . . .

ED

(*Less frightened*)

Aw, stay an' warm yourself, Phoebe, an' don't mind Jake. He's sort of queer hisself, I reckon.

(*They watch as* PHOEBE *pulls the bench nearer to the fire and settles herself, crouched over the warmth. They sit down as far away from her as possible but* ED *and* UNCLE BENNY *are still uneasy. Thunder is heard.*)

PHOEBE

Gibbie, you been a-wrigglin' 'round an' hoppin'. Don't be signin' me to go right yet. Jest leave me set a spell an' get a rest an' warmin'. Set still, Gibbie, set still, set still. . . .

UNCLE BENNY

(*Staring fascinated at the toad*)

I don't like these here goin's-on, I don't. I don't like that varmint of hers!

ED

I sure wish that ol' toad would hop off from here an' sign the hag she's got to move on. I hope to God this here *is* the last time for ol' Phoebe!

PHOEBE

(*Lies down on the bench*)

Set still, Gibbie, set still.

UNCLE BENNY

(*Quavering*)

I—I don't like to stay in this place, Jake. 'Tain't no good luck comin' from three lights in a room an' I'm feared of that varmint. It's a demon, sure. One of us'll be witched if we stays! Let's us go!

JAKE

(*Shaking off any fears and speaking with studied gruffness. Rolling thunder is heard.*)

An' let the screechin' devils get you from the clouds!

ED

That ol' toad makes my flesh crawl. Somethin's goin' to happen!

JAKE

Aw, come on, boys. I ain't goin' to let this here hag an' her dirty ol' toad spoil my good liquor. I'm goin' to have a drink. (*He fills the jug and pours more whiskey in the mugs. As he goes to the corner to the big jug he looks defiantly at* PHOEBE.) She's done gone to sleep as peaceful as you please. (*He sits down to drink and the others recover a little.*) I ain't goin' to let ol' Phoebe witch me. I ain't feared of her.

ED

(*Looking intently at* JAKE)

They do say as how witches cain't harm them as is

like themselves. (*Insinuating.*) They do say they's men witches, too.

JAKE

(*Begins to show drunken bravado. He speaks sarcastically.*)

Well, now, mebbe I am a witch. I ain't never thought about it before. I never did know jest how to call myself, but mebbe that's jest what I am, a witch. (*Laughing, with a swagger at* UNCLE BENNY.) You'd better look out for me, Benny!

UNCLE BENNY

Aw, now, Jake, I ain't never done nothin' agin' you, Jake. Now you know I ain't, Jake.

ED

(*Half maliciously*)

They do say there's somethin' queer when a man ain't a-feared of a witch an' her demon.

JAKE

Naw, I ain't feared of her. (*He takes another drink. All show the effects of the liquor.*) An' I'll tell you-all what I'll do. I'll go right up to the old hag an' snatch that cap right off'n her head, I will!

(*He rises.*)

ED

They do say she keeps a heap of money in that ol' bonnet o' hers.

UNCLE BENNY

(*He rises*)

Don't tech her, Jake. Don't rile her. Leave her

be. (*As* JAKE *advances to the bench where* PHOEBE *lies.*) Aw, Jake!

JAKE

I'll see if this here ol' bundle is full o' demon witch-spells or jest good money.

(*He puts out his hand toward the cap.*)

UNCLE BENNY

(*Jumps up, trembling with horror, as a crash of thunder is heard outside.*)

Don't, Jake! Look at that witch! Look thar! That ain't nothin' but her skin layin' thar. See how shrivelled 'tis. Oh, lordy, Jake. She's done already slipped out'n her hide an' she's ridin' through the sky. She left her skin behind! (*With despair.*) Oh, lordy, lordy.

JAKE

Aw, drat you, Benny. Quit your shriekin'. You'll jump out'n your own skin next. This here's Phoebe Ward an' all of her, too,—(*With a swagger*)—an' I'll show you! (*Before* UNCLE BENNY *can stop him he reaches out and lays a finger on* PHOEBE'S *hand. He draws back, awestruck.*) Wal, I'll be damned! (*Touches her again.*) My God, Benny, if she ain't dead! Get a lookin' glass, Ed. (ED *brings a cracked glass from the mantel shelf.* JAKE *holds it before* PHOEBE'S *mouth.*) Yes, sir, sure's you're born, Phoebe Ward's done blew out. She's had her last ride for sure.

UNCLE BENNY

(*Wildly entreating*)

Cover her up, Jake. Cover her up! I don't want to see her no more. Them three lights was a sign. Oh, lordy, lordy!

JAKE

(*Goes to the door and pulls down the old sheet, throws it over* PHOEBE)

Thar, now, that'll do. (*He goes to the table and drains his glass.*) Here, brace up, all, an' have a drink.

(*They drink in silence.*)

ED

Wal, she's gone.

JAKE

Say, you-all, ol' Phoebe's dead an' I reckon we might's well drink her wake right now. Fill up, all.

(ED *pours the whiskey while* JAKE *takes the candles from the table and places two at the head and one at the feet of the "corpse."*

ED

(*Gulping*)

Here's you, Jake!

(*He drinks.*)

JAKE

Here's to ol' Phoebe.

(*He drinks, laughing coarsely.*)

UNCLE BENNY

Oh, Lord, help us.

(*He drinks.*)

ED

This place's gettin' cold—needs some more wood on the fire.

(*The fire has burned low and the light is dim.*)

JAKE

Wal, *you* put it on.

ED

(*Solemnly*)

I wouldn't go nigh that there witch's corpse, not if her ol' cap was plumb full of gold!

JAKE

Aw, I'd shake hands with her ol' man, the Devil hisself, to-night.

(JAKE *gets up and goes around the bench to the woodpile, with his back to the "corpse."* PHOEBE *sits up, very slowly, and feebly pushes aside the shroud. The thunder is heard above the storm outside. The shutter bangs and the candles are puffed out.* JAKE *drops his load of wood into the fire and turns toward the bench as he hears the sound behind him. He leans against the side of the fireplace. All stand spellbound, gazing at the witch.*)

Scene from *When Witches Ride*, a play of folk-superstition, by Elizabeth Lay. PHOEBE WARD (Alga E. Leavitt); ED (Le Grand Everett); JAKE (George Denny); and UNCLE BENNY (George Mc. F. McKie).

PHOEBE: Uncle Benny, gimme a drap o' liquor. It's mighty cold over here. I'm done frizzed clean through . . . . jest one little drap . . . . before I go! This here's my last time!

PHOEBE

Uncle Benny, gimme a drap o' liquor. It's mighty cold over here. (*Shivering, she gets up and shuffles toward the table.* ED *and* UNCLE BENNY *retreat in horror.*) I'm done frizzed clean through . . . jest one little drap . . . before I go! This here's my last time! (*She picks up a cup and gulps hurriedly as if fearful that she will be forced to go before it is finished.*) This here's my last time!

JAKE

(*Infuriated*)

This here's your last time, is it? Warn't you dead? Ain't we done drunk your wake? Ain't it time to bury you now? You git yourself out'n that thar door, Phoebe Ward! You're dead for sure an' I'm going to bury you now.

(*The storm outside grows fiercer, with the heavy sound of thunder. Flashes of lightning are seen through the window as the shutter swings in the wind.*)

PHOEBE

(*Menacingly to* JAKE)

You'd best to leave me be, Jake! 'Tain't in your hands to dig a grave whar Phoebe'll lie. 'Twon't be no good that'll follow him as sees me ride the clouds to-night!

JAKE

(*Frenzied, he dashes her aside and strides to the door*)

You won't ride the clouds no more'n I will, you

damned witch! You're dead an' it's time you're buried! (*He stumbles through the door.*) Come on out, or I'll come back an' drag you out when I get your grave dug.

(*Vivid lightning is seen through the door as* JAKE *strides out. Loud crashes of thunder sound near by.*)

PHOEBE

(*Exalted, listening as she moves to the door*)

Oh, I hear the Black Uns thunderin' down the pathways of the sky! I hear 'em whirlin' through the clouds an' dartin' flames of fire! It's all of hell is risin' up to carry me away! (*Strong wind and rolling thunder are heard.*) Oh, they're screamin' out for Phoebe an' they're wild to sweep her through the storm with the Devil at her side! 'Tis the Devil hisself is waitin' an' he's scorchin' up the blackness with the lightnin's of his eyes! (*As though in answer to a call from without.*) I'm comin', I'm comin'! I'll be ridin'! I'll be ridin'!

(*She stands in the open door, facing the room, and a terrific flash of lightning throws her figure into dark silhouette. Then she retreats backward and the door bangs behind her.* UNCLE BENNY *and* ED *are left crouching by the table.*)

UNCLE BENNY

She's gone. She'll get Jake.

Ed

Oh, Lord, where's her toad? Where's her sperit?

(There is a wild crack and crash of thunder, the door bangs open and there is another blinding flash of lightning. Jake *stumbles through the door in terrible fright. His hands are over his eyes, as if he is blinded. He gropes, stumbling, to the table and falls into a seat.)*

Jake

(Stunned)

I seen 'im! I seen 'im!

Uncle Benny

My Lord!

Ed

What— What was it, Jake?

Jake

(Wildly)

I'm witched! Oh, I seen all the Black Uns in Hell, I seen the Devil hisself! I seen 'im, I seen the Ol' Man! The heavens done opened like a blazin', roarin' furnace an' the storm clouds wrapped ol' Phoebe 'round an' snatched her up in fire! An' all the clawin' demons out'n Hell rid roarin' past my ears. Oh, they've blinded me with balls of fire an' knocked me to the ground. An' the Devil hisself done carried off ol' Phoebe for to ride among the witches. I seen 'im, I done seen 'im!

ED

My God, he seen the Devil! He's witched sure.

UNCLE BENNY

(*Moves back trembling and steps against the toad, which has moved near to the table. He jumps in fright and stares at it in horror.*

Oh, good Lord, the spell's here!

ED

What do you see?

UNCLE BENNY

The toad!

JAKE

My God! She left her toad!

ED

It's done moved! It's moved from where she put it.

UNCLE BENNY

Her spell's passed on Jake. Her demon's witched him! Oh, lordy!

JAKE

It's moved, it's moved! (*Struggling as with a spell.*) Oh, I got to go too. The witch's toad's done got me an' I got to go. (*Retreating from the toad with his hands to his eyes as before.*) I'm goin', Gibbie, I'm goin', I'm goin'. . . .

(*He turns at the door and stumbles out into the night. The door remains open on blackness and a roaring wind blows through the room, leaving it nearly in darkness as* ED *and* UNCLE BENNY *stare at the toad and retreat in horror.*)

ED

It done got him!

UNCLE BENNY

The Devil took him! Oh, Lord, help us. Oh, lordy, lordy!

(ED *and* UNCLE BENNY *fall on their knees and crouch in abject terror. The sound of thunder is heard rolling in the distance.*)

CURTAIN

PEGGY[1]

A Tragedy of the Tenant Farmer

BY

HAROLD WILLIAMSON

PEGGY

CAST OF CHARACTERS

As originally produced at The Play-House, Chapel Hill, North Carolina, May 30 and 31, 1919.

WILL WARREN, *a tenant farmer,* George McF. McKie
MAG WARREN, *his wife,* Elizabeth Taylor
PEGGY, *their daughter, aged 18,* Virginia McFadyen
HERMAN, *their son, aged 6,* Nat Henry
JED, *a farm hand, in love with Peggy,* Harold Williamson
JOHN McDONALD, *the landowner,* George Denny
WESLEY McDONALD, *his son, a University student* George Crawford

SCENE: A tenant farm in North Carolina. The bare living-room of a two-room cabin.

TIME: The present. An April evening, about seven o'clock.

SCENE

THE scene is laid in one of the two rooms of a tenant shack. In the centre of the room is a square eating-table with an oil-cloth cover. On each side of the table is a straw-bottom chair. A small, worn cook-stove is in the left corner and beside it a wood-box. At the right of the store is a rectangular table on which are a dishpan and other cooking utensils. Against the back wall is a cupboard which holds the meagre supply of tableware. On top of it are several paper sacks and pasteboard boxes containing cooking materials. A door in the right side leads from the eating-room into the only other room of the shack, used as a sleeping-room. A door at the back on the left leads outdoors. Through this doorway can be seen a crude string lattice-work partly covered by a growing vine, and a shelf supporting a bucket and gourd. A small window is at the right in the back wall. The floor and walls are bare. Everything has a fairly neat appearance but suggests the struggle against a degrading poverty.

As the curtain rises MAG WARREN *is busily preparing supper, singing as she works.* HERMAN *is sitting on the floor tying a piece of rope to the end of a broom handle.*

MAG WARREN *is a thin, bent, overworked woman of forty-two. Her face reveals the strain of years of drudgery. Her thin hair is drawn tightly into a knot on the back of her head. She wears a cheap calico dress and a faded checkered apron. In the pocket of her apron is a large snuff can. A protruding snuff-brush claims the right corner of her mouth.*[1]*. She beats up a*

Mag's Song

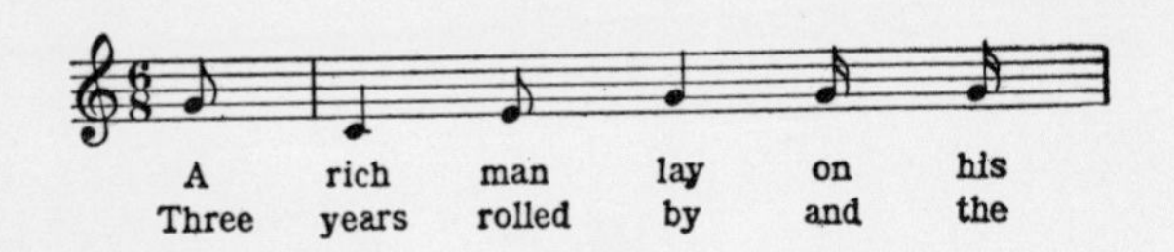

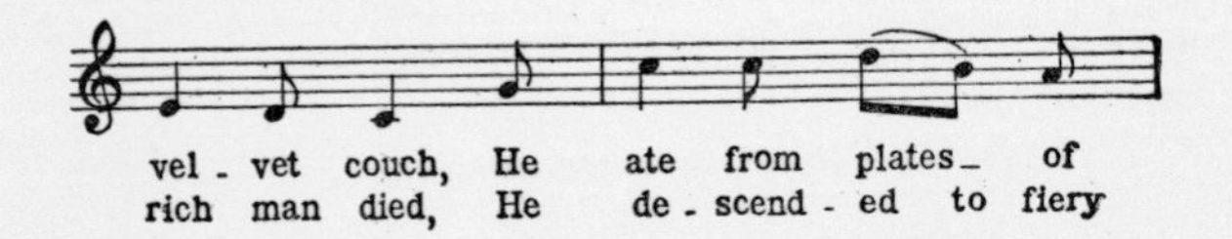

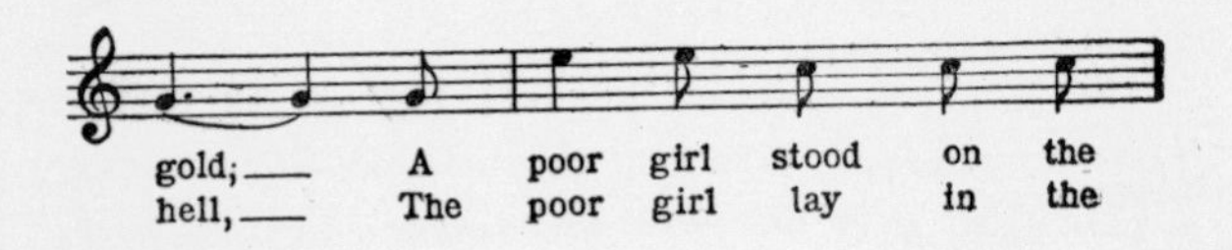

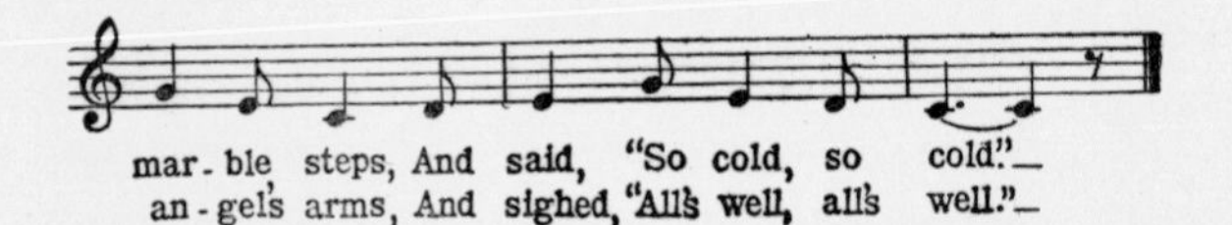

1 The habit of "dipping snuff" is common among the poor whites in all sections of North Carolina. A twig is chewed into shreds at one end and is known as a snuff-stick or "tooth-brush." This is dipped

batter of cornbread, pours it into a pan on the stove, and after pouring some water into a large coffee-pot, she begins to slice some "fatback." [1]

Herman is an under-sized boy of six years with a vacant expression on his pinched face. He wears a faded shirt, and a lone suspender over his right shoulder gives scanty support for his patched pants, which strike him midway between the knee and the ankle. He is barefooted. When he finishes fixing his "horse," he gets up, straddles the stick, and trots over all the unoccupied part of the room.

HERMAN

Git up, Kit . . . whoa . . . ha. (*Whipping the stick.*) What's the matter? Cain't you plow straight?

(*In his trotting he runs into* MAG *at the stove. She turns on him angrily.*)

MAG

Git out'n my way an' git over thar in the corner. (*Utterly subdued,* HERMAN *goes and sits in the corner while* MAG *goes on with her work. Presently she turns to him.*) Go git me a turn o' wood, an' don't you take all day about it neither.

(HERMAN *goes out.* MAG *continues to sing, moving about between the table, stove, and cup-*

into the powdered snuff and then rubbed over the gums and teeth. The women seem to get much satisfaction from this practice.

1 "Fatback" is fat salt pork which, together with cornbread, forms the main part of the diet of "hog and hominy" eaten by poor whites the year 'round.

board as she prepares the meal. JED SMITH *enters. He is a tall, lanky, uncanny-looking fellow of twenty-four. He is dressed in the shabby shirt and faded blue overalls of an ordinary poor farm-laborer. He walks in slowly and lazily and says nothing. As he goes to the table* MAG *looks up at him from her work.*)

MAG

I thought you was Will, Jed. (*She continues her work.*) Seen anything o' Pegg? Hit's a-gittin' mighty high time she's back here.

JED

(*Pulls out a chair from the table, flops down in it, and begins whittling on a stick*)

That's what I come to see you about, Mag.

MAG

(*Stopping her work and looking around at* JED)

Ain't nothin' happened, air there, Jed?

JED

Nothin' to git skeered about, but ol' man McDonald's boy come in from one o' them 'air colleges th' other day an' I jest seen Pegg down yonder a-talkin' to him an' a-lookin' at him mighty sweet-like. 'Tain't the fust time neither.

MAG

(*Goes up nearer to* JED)

So that's what's been a-keepin' her?

JED

Yeah, an' if you don't watch out, Mag, there's a tale goin' to git out an' ol' man McDonald'll drive you off'n the place.

MAG

You're right, Jed. Jest wait till me an' her pa gits through with her. We'll put a stop to it.

JED

(*Nervously*)

Now don't go an' tell her I told you, Mag.

MAG

You needn't be skeered. I been a-thinkin' as much myself. She's been powerful uppity lately, but I didn't know what about. Her pa's allus said that perty face o' hern would be the ruinin' of her. Don't you know Wes McDonald wouldn't be a-havin' nothin' to do with Pegg 'lessen she was perty?

JED

Naw.

MAG

She's clear out'n his class an' ain't got sense enough to know it. (*She turns the corn cake in the pan.*) An' it's a perty way she's a-doin' you, Jed.

JED

(*Drearily*)

Yeah, I reckon she ain't likin' me no more.

(HERMAN *returns with the wood and throws it in the box.*)

MAG

Ain't she said she'd marry you?

JED

Aw, she did onc't.

MAG

An' you're a good match for her, too. Will's a-been a-sayin' how good you are at the plow.

JED

I'd shore like to have her, Mag.

MAG

Well, if you want her you can git her, Jed. She's done a right smart o' washin' an' a-cookin' an' a-hoein' in her day an' I reckon she'll make you a good woman.

JED

I ain't a-worryin' about that.

MAG

(*Looking out of the window*)

Yonder she comes now. Ain't no tellin' what fool notions that boy has been a-puttin' in her head, but you jest wait till me an' her pa gits through with her.

JED

(*Rising nervously*)

Reckon I'll be a-goin' now, Mag.

MAG

Ain't you goin' to wait an' see Pegg? 'Pears like you'd be a-pushin' yourself.

JED

Naw, I . . . I'll come back after I eat.

MAG

Well, you come back. Me an' her pa'll have her in a notion then.

HERMAN

(*Stops* JED *as he is going out*)

Gimme some terbaccer, Jed.

JED

(*Feels in his pockets*)

I ain't got none, Herman.

(*He goes out.*)

MAG

What'd I tell you about axin' folks for terbaccer? When you want terbaccer ax your pa for it.

HERMAN

He won't gimme none.

MAG

Well, it don't make no odds. You don't do nothin' but waste it nohow.

(HERMAN *sits down on the floor to the front and begins to play aimlessly.*

PEGGY *comes in, flushed and happy. She is a pretty girl of eighteen years. She has attractive features, is of medium height, slim and lively. Her hair is light and becomingly disheveled. Her dress is extremely simple but shows signs of care.*)

PEGGY

Supper ready, ma?

MAG

Cain't you see it ain't? Why ain't you been here long ago a-helpin' me to git supper?

PEGGY

(*Putting the milk bucket she has brought in with her on the table, she goes over to the left to hang up her bonnet.*)

I couldn't finish milkin' no sooner.

MAG

You needn't tell me you been a-milkin' all this time. Where you been anyhow?

PEGGY

I stopped to help Lizzie Taylor hang out her wash.

MAG

Been anywheres else?

PEGGY

No'm.

MAG

Well, git busy a-fixin' that table, an' tell me what fool notions Wes McDonald's been a-puttin' into your head.

PEGGY

(*She tries to look surprised*)

I don't know nothin' 'bout Wes McDonald, ma.

MAG

Don't you lie to your ma like that, Pegg. You think I don't know nothin' 'bout it, but you cain't fool your ma. He's been a-settin' up to you, ain't he?

PEGGY

No, ma, he ain't said nothin' to me, he . . .

MAG

Now be keerful.

PEGGY

He jest spoke to me, an' I jest axed him how he liked to go off to school an' he said he liked it an' he axed me why I wasn't goin' to school an' I told him I had to work.

MAG

Didn't he say nothin' 'bout your bein' perty?

PEGGY

(*Proudly*)

Yes, he said I was perty. Said if I had book-learnin' an' lived uptown I'd be the pick o' the whole bunch.

MAG

That's what I was a-thinkin' he'd be a-puttin' into your head. You keep out'n Wes McDonald's way. He ain't a-keerin' nothin' for you and besides he'll git you into trouble. Wait till your pa hears o' this.

(*There is a silence while* MAG *goes on with her work.*)

PEGGY

(*Looking out of the window, wistfully*)

I reckon it'd be nice to go to school.

MAG

Mebbe it is. If you'd a-been rich, schoolin' might a-done you some good, but you ain't rich an' schoolin's only for them as is rich. Me an' your pa never had no schoolin', and I reckon you can git along 'thout any yourself. (*She goes to the door and looks off anxiously across the fields.*) Hit's high time your pa was a-gittin' home.

HERMAN

I'd like to see pa myself. Want some terbaccer.

MAG

(*Comes to the front. Solemnly*)

I been mighty skeered 'bout your pa ever since the doctor told him he had that 'air misery round his heart.

PEGGY

Did he say 'twas dangerous?

MAG

(*Going back to the stove*)

Well, he said your pa was liable to keel over most any time if he ain't mighty keerful. Ol' man McDonald's got him down yonder in that 'air new ground a-bustin' roots an' it ain't a-doin' your pa no good neither.

PEGGY

I jest seen pa an' Mr. McDonald a-talkin' together an' both of 'em was mighty mad about somethin'.

MAG

I reckon your pa struck him for a raise, an' he ought to have it. A dollar an' a quarter a day ain't enough, workin' like your pa does, but ol' man McDonald'd see your pa clear to hell afore he'd pay him a cent more. (*She goes to the door, takes the snuff-brush from her mouth and spits out the snuff. She puts the snuff-brush in her pocket, takes a drink of water from the gourd and washes her mouth out with it, spitting out the water. She speaks to* PEGGY *as she turns back to the stove.*) There's them cabbages your pa told you to hoe an' you ain't done it, have you?

PEGGY

No, ma, I ain't had time.

MAG

You had a-plenty o' time to let Wes McDonald put a lot o' fool notions in your head. You'll have a perty time a-tellin' your pa you ain't had time. (*There is a pause.*) Jed said as how he might come around after he's eat. Hit's a perty way you been a-treatin' Jed an' he ain't a-likin' it neither.

PEGGY

I don't care if he likes it or not. 'Tain't none o' his business.

MAG

Hit ain't? Ain't you done told him you was a-goin' to marry him?

PEGGY

I might have onc't, but I've changed my mind.

MAG

(*Angrily*)

What's come over you anyhow?

PEGGY

Nothin', ma.

MAG

Well, I'd like to know what you think you're a-goin' to do? 'Tain't every man a woman can git, an' you ought to thank the Lord Jed's given you the chanct.

PEGGY

I ain't a-wantin' it. I ain't a-goin' to marry Jed an' have to work like a dog all my life—besides, I got to love the man I marry.

MAG

(*Scornfully*)

Love? What's love got to do with your bread an' meat? You been a-readin' some o' them magazines as they git down at the house. I'd like to know what you think you're goin' to do?

PEGGY

(*Resolved*)

I'm goin' to git me a job up town an' *be* somebody!

MAG

There ain't nothin' you could do there. You was raised on a farm, an' I reckon that's jest about the place for you. You don't think you're better'n your ma, do you?

PEGGY

No, ma, but I could git me a job in the Five an' Ten Cent Store. Mary Cameron's got her a job there, an' she's a-wearin' fine clothes an' got a lot o' fellows.

MAG

Yes, an' there's a lot a-bein' said as to how she got them clothes. I tell you, me an' your pa ain't a-goin' to have nothin' like that.

PEGGY

But, ma, I——

MAG

Shet up. You behave yourself like you ought ta before Jed. If you don't, you better.

PEGGY

I'll treat him all right but I ain't a-goin' to marry him.

MAG

Me an' your pa'll say if you will or not, an'——

PEGGY

The bread's a-burnin', ma!

MAG

(*Running quickly across the room she jerks the bread off the stove and dumps it into a pan on the table*)

Good Lord, now don't that beat you? An' there ain't no more meal. (*She looks out of the door.*) Yonder comes your pa, too. Hurry up an' git that table laid while I git a bucket o' water.

(*She takes the pail and hurries off.*

WILL WARREN *comes in heavily. He is a slouchy, hump-shouldered man of fifty years. His hair is long and his face unshaven. He wears an old, dirty, sweat-ridden black hat with a shaggy brim; a faded blue denim shirt; brown corduroy pants, worn slick, attached to a large pair of suspenders by nails; and brogan shoes with heavy gray socks falling over the top. He drags himself in and stands propped against the side of the door. His face is white and he appears entirely exhausted.*)

HERMAN

(Going up to WILL*)*

Gimme some terbaccer, pa. (WILL *pays no attention to him.)* Pa, gimme some terbaccer.

WILL

(Giving HERMAN *a slap on the face that sends him to the floor)*

Git to hell away from me.

(He comes into the room slowly and unsteadily, pulls off his hat and throws it into the corner, and falls into a chair by the table, breathing heavily and staring blankly. He says nothing.)

PEGGY

(She notices WILL'S *heavy breathing and is alarmed.)*

What's the matter, pa, ain't you feelin' well?

WILL

(Struggling for breath)

Gimme . . . some coffee . . . quick!

PEGGY

(Quickly pouring a cup of coffee and giving it to him. He gulps it down and appears considerably relieved)

You ain't sick, air you, pa?

WILL

Naw. . . . It's another one o' them durned miseries round my heart. *(He gulps the coffee.)* I ain't a-goin' to work another day in that durned new ground. I told McDonald I wouldn't an' damned if I do.

MAG

(*Who has now come back, and has overheard his words*)

I don't blame you for sayin' so, but there ain't no use in flyin' off'n the handle like that.

WILL

Well, I said it an' I'll do it. These here money men like McDonald think as how they can work a poor man like me to death an' pay me nothin' for it neither, but durned if I don't show him.

MAG

What'd he say when you axed him for a raise?

WILL

Aw, he said he was a-losin' money every year. He allus says that. Says he ain't a-raisin' enough to pay for the growin' of it, but don't you reckon I know how much he's a raisin'? He's a-gittin' thirty cents a pound for his cotton an' two dollars a bushel for his corn, an' then he says he ain't a-makin' nothin'. He cain't lie to me, he's a-gittin' rich.

MAG

Course he is. Ain't he jest bought another one o' them automobiles th' other day?

WILL

Yeah, an' while him an' that no'count boy o' his'n are a-ridin' around in it I'm down yonder in that 'air new ground a-gittin' a dollar an' a quarter a day for killin' myself over them durned roots. Jest afore quittin' time I come mighty nigh givin' out.

MAG

(*She brings the cornbread and "fatback" and puts it on the table.* PEGGY *busies herself at the table and cupboard*)

You better take keer o' yourself. You know what the doctor told you.

WILL

Yeah, but how in the devil can I help it like things are now? I told him what's what a while ago, an' damned if I don't stick to it too. (*He looks over the table.*) What you got for supper? (*Seeing the burnt bread, he picks it up and hurls it to the floor.*) What kind o' durned cookin' do you call this you're doin', anyway?

MAG

It wouldn't a-happened if Pegg hadn't been a-pesterin' me.

WILL

(*Angrily to* PEGGY)

Well, what you been a-doin'?

PEGGY

Nothin', pa.

MAG

In the fust place, you told her to hoe them cabbages.

WILL

Ain't you done it?

MAG

No, she ain't done it, but she's been down yonder a-lettin' Wes McDonald put a lot o' fool notions into her head about her bein' perty, an' now she says she ain't a-going to marry Jed.

WILL

(*Savagely to* PEGGY)

You ain't, air you?

PEGGY

(*Half crying but defiant*)

No, pa, I ain't. I've seen you an' ma a-workin' from sun-up to sun-down like niggers an' jest a-makin' enough to keep us out'n the poor house, an' I ain't a-going to live no sich life with Jed. He couldn't do no better.

WILL

Well, durn your hide . . .

MAG

An' she says she'll git her a job up-town like Mary Cameron's got. You know what's a-bein' said about Mary! (*To* PEGGY.) Don't you know we ain't a-goin' to have nothin' like that?

(*She shakes her finger at* PEGGY.)

PEGGY

But, ma, I . . .

WILL

Shet up. We've raised you up here an' it's us as'll say what you'll do. Jed axed you to marry him an' durn it, you'll do it, too.

PEGGY

I won't.

WILL

(*Rising from the chair*)

You won't? Don't you let me hear you say that agin.

PEGGY

(*Wildly*)

I won't, I won't, I won't!

WILL

(*In uncontrolled rage*)

Then, damn you, you can git right out'n this house right now an' . . .

MAG

Hush, Will, hush.

WILL

(*Breathing heavily and struggling in his speech*)

An' don't you . . . let . . . me ever . . . see you . . . agin . . .

(*Clutching his hands to his heart, he gasps, staggers backward, then falls heavily to the floor. The women stand stunned for a moment, then* MAG *rushes over, kneels by him, and shakes him.*)

MAG

Will, Will, . . . answer me, Will, . . . say somethin'. (*Turning to* PEGGY, *who has not moved, and speaking dully.*) Lord, Pegg, he's dead, . . . your pa's dead . . . he's gone. Send for somebody . . . quick!

PEGGY

(*Excitedly to* HERMAN)

Run tell Mister McDonald to come here quick. He's down at the house. Go git him quick! (HERMAN *runs out.* MAG, *shaking with sobs, crouches over the body. Her head is buried in her apron.* PEGGY *tries to comfort her mother.*) Don't carry on like that, ma. It ain't a-doin' no good. (*Hopefully.*) Mebbe he ain't dead.

MAG

Yes, he is. He's gone. . . . Oh, Lord . . . I knowed it'd git him.

(JED *appears at the door and stands stupefied for a moment.*)

JED

(*Coming into the room*)

What's the matter? (*Going nearer to the body.*) What's the matter with Will?

MAG

He's gone, Jed, he's gone. O Lord!

JED

He ain't dead, is he? Who done it?

(JED *kneels over the body and examines it for signs of life.* MAG *rises slowly, shuffles to a chair on the other side of the table and sits sobbing.*)

PEGGY

(*Appealing*)

Is he dead, Jed, is he dead?

JED

I don't know. Git some camphor, quick.

(PEGGY *runs into the other room for the camphor bottle.*

JOHN MCDONALD *enters, followed by his* son, WESLEY. *The farm-owner is a tall, prosperous-looking man of forty-eight. He has a hard face and stern, overbearing manner.*

WESLEY *is a rather handsome young fellow of twenty-one, a typical well-dressed college boy.*)

MCDONALD

(*To* JED, *taking in the scene at a glance*)

What's the matter? Is he dead?

JED

(*Rising*)

I believe he is, Mister McDonald.

McDONALD

How did it happen?

JED

I don't know.

MAG

(*Sobbing*)

He's gone, Mister McDonald, he's gone. . . . He had another one of them fits with his heart jest like the doctor said he would, an' he went all of a sudden afore I knowed it.

McDONALD

(*Examining the body*)

Well, he's dead all right, sure. (*Peggy runs in with the camphor bottle.*) That's no use, he's dead. Jed, let's put him on the bed in the other room.

(*They carry the body off the stage,* MAG *following.*)

WESLEY

I'm awfully sorry, Peggy. Tell me how it happened.

PEGGY

(*Crying*)

He got mad with me because I said I wouldn't marry Jed, an' he jest got madder an' madder an' told me to leave an' never come back. An' then he put his hands up to his heart like this, an' fell over.

WESLEY

Did he have heart trouble?

PEGGY

Yeah, I reckon so. He's been a-havin' pains in his side, an' a-chokin' for wind, an' the doctor said he'd have to be keerful.

WESLEY

And he wanted you to marry Jed?

PEGGY

Yeah, he said I'd have to.

WESLEY

(*Understandingly*)

And you didn't want to?

PEGGY

No, if I married him I'd have to work like a dog all my life, an' I ain't a-goin' to do it.

WESLEY

I don't blame you, Peggy, but what are you going to do?

PEGGY

I'm goin' to git me a job up-town.

WESLEY

You mustn't go there, Peggy. You couldn't get along there.

PEGGY

(*Looking to him wistfully*)

Well, what can I do?

WESLEY

(*Thoughtfully*)

I don't know. . . . I guess you'd better marry Jed. (*There is a pause.* PEGGY *goes over to the window and looks out hopelessly.*) If everything was different I'd . . . Oh, I didn't mean that. You see such a thing would be impossible.

PEGGY

(*Turning to him, hopefully*)

But I could . . .

WESLEY

Stop, Peggy. . . . I think a lot of you but don't you see I couldn't do more? It's impossible. Don't cry that way, Peggy. I'm sorry I said what I did this afternoon. I didn't mean to upset you like this. Go on and marry Jed. He's all right and I'll see that he gets a good showing.

PEGGY

(*Desperately*)

But I don't want to. I know how it'll turn out.

(MCDONALD *and* JED *return, followed by* MAG.)

MAG

(*Without hope*)

What's a-goin' to come of us now?

McDONALD

(*Brusquely*)

I don't know, Mag.

MAG

You ain't a-goin' to make us leave, air you?

McDONALD

Let's not talk about that now.

MAG

But tell me, Mister McDonald, will we have to leave?

McDONALD

(*Impatient*)

Well, if you just must know right now, Mag, I'm sorry to say it, but I don't see how I can keep you here.

MAG

(*Imploring him*)

For God's sake don't make us leave the place!

McDONALD

Now don't get foolish, Mag. You see it's a business proposition with me. With Will gone there's nothing you and your family could do on the farm that would pay me to keep you here. It's the man I need, especially now when there is so much plowing to be done, and as soon as I can I will have to get another man to take Will's place. Of course he will have to live in this house.

MAG

(*Resentful*)

After Will has worked for you steady for sixteen year you ain't a-goin' to turn me out now, air you?

McDONALD

I'm sorry if you look at it in that way, Mag, but business is business, and I can't afford to keep you here.

MAG

But, Mister McDonald, we ain't got nowhere else to go . . . an' we'd starve to death.

(*She turns away sobbing.*)

McDONALD

You ought to be thankful for what I've done for Will. He was about the sorriest hand I ever had. There's absolutely nothing you can do. I can't keep you.

WESLEY

But, father, you can't turn them away like this.

McDONALD

It's time you were learning that business is not a charitable institution, Wesley. I'm trying to run a farm, not a hard-luck asylum.

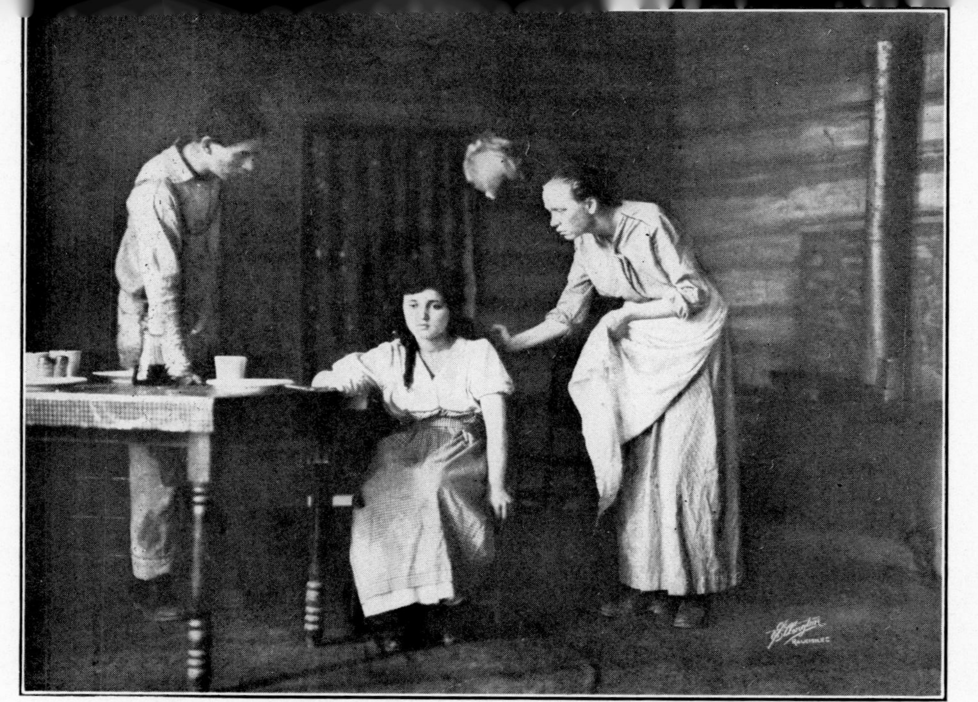

Scene from *Peggy*, a tragedy of the tenant farmer, by Harold Williamson, who also takes the part of JED in the play, with PEGGY (Virginia McFadden) and MAG (Elizabeth Taylor).

MAG: You'll marry Jed, won't you, Pegg? You ain't a-goin' to see your ol' ma go to the poorhouse, air you, Pegg?

PEGGY: I reckon . . . . it's the only way . . . . for me.

JED

Mister McDonald, let me see you a minute.

(*He goes over and whispers to* McDONALD.)

McDONALD

(*To* JED)

Well, if you do that everything will be all right! (PEGGY *looks up hopefully. He turns to* MAG.) Jed has just said that if Peggy would marry him he will let you and the boy stay here in the house with them. If you want to do that it will be all right with me.

(PEGGY, *disheartened, sits down by the table and buries her head in her arms, crying.*)

MAG

You'll marry Jed, won't you, Pegg? You'll do it for your ma, won't you?

McDONALD

Well, I'll leave that for you to decide. You can let me know later. (*Going to the door.*) Come, Wesley. I'll send to town for something to put him in, and Jed can get help to dig the grave. If you want anything, let me know.

(McDONALD *and* WESLEY *go out.* WESLEY *hesitates in the door a moment, looking with sympathy at* PEGGY).

JED

(*He goes slowly and uneasily over to* PEGGY)

You ain't a-goin' to turn me down, air you, Peggy?

MAG

(*Imploring*)

You'll marry Jed, won't you, Pegg? You ain't a-goin' to see your ol' ma go to the poorhouse, air you, Pegg?

PEGGY

(*After a moment of silence she raises her head and speaks in broken sobs*)

I reckon . . . it's the only way . . . for me.

CURTAIN

"DOD GAST YE BOTH!"[1]

A Comedy of Mountain Moonshiners

BY

HUBERT C. HEFFNER

"DOD GAST YE BOTH!"

CAST OF CHARACTERS

As originally produced at The Play-House, Chapel Hill, North Carolina, April 30 and May 1, 1920.

NOAH SETZER, *a mountain moonshiner,* George Denny
WALT, *his son, an ex-member of the A.E.F.,* Wilbur Stout
MARY, *his daughter,* Ione Markham
BILL SPIVINS, *a rough mountaineer,* Bergin Lohr
MOSE, } *frequenters of the still and* { Chester Burton
SANK, } *bootleggers for Noah* { Hubert Heffner
LAURENCE ABNER, *a "revenoor,"* George Crawford

SCENE: A dense thicket in the mountains of North Carolina.

TIME: Four o'clock in the morning. The spring of 1919.

SCENE

A TYPICAL mountain moonshiner's retreat in a remote cove in the mountains of western North Carolina.

The whole scene is hedged in on all sides by a thicket of tall rhododendron. At the back runs a small, trickling brook which supplies the water for distilling purposes. On the left is the still proper, to the right at the rear, the mash tub. Boards are nailed between some of the trees to form rough benches. Near the front of the stage three modern, high-powered rifles are stacked against a tree. The ground immediately around the still shows signs of much tramping.

When the curtain rises WALT *is discovered, standing by the mash tub, leaning idly on his paddle and smoking a cigarette.* SANK *is stretched out on a bench at the right, fast asleep and snoring loudly.* MOSE *sprawls on the ground near the still, smoking an old cob pipe.*

MOSE *is a heavy-set, rough mountaineer. He is dressed in a blue shirt, patched coat, and dirty khaki pants, stuffed into heavy laced boots. There is almost a week's growth of stubby beard on his face.*

SANK *is a thin, shriveled old man of about sixty years, so bent as to appear little. He is dressed in dirty khaki trousers, blue shirt, worn coat and heavy shoes, with blue knit socks hanging down over his shoe-tops. His beard is very scant—thin as is his shrill effeminate voice.*

WALT *is a lank, lazy-looking fellow of about twenty-two. An ex-member of the A. E. F., he still wears his overseas cap and military breeches.*

WALT

(*Looking at his heavy turnip watch*)

'Bout four o'clock. Soon be through. So the cops give ye a hard run of it, did they, Mose?

(*He stirs the mash.*)

MOSE

Yeah, since that thar pro-ser-ser-bition . . . they're gittin' tighter'n a rum jug. I used to could take a run o' brandy to Lenore an' measure hit out right on the streets, but ye can't do it no more.

WALT

Guess ye took the preachers their half o' gallon per, all right, did ye?

MOSE

(*Speaking with a drawl, between the puffs of his pipe*)

Yeah, ever' sanctified one of 'em. They can't preach their hell fire and brimstone sermonts if they ain't got their fiery spirits. Hit's about time th' ol' man was comin' back. He's had time to send in the watchers, an' he seemed to be so anxious to finish up an' go home. Ye'd better git to stirrin' that mash.

WALT

(*Smoking idly*)

Oh, well. Mary'll meet th' ol' man if she went by the back way. What ye reckon she came fer, anyway,

Mose? 'Tain't nothin' here she wanted this time o' night, an' she didn't git nothin'.

MOSE

Dunno. (*He puffs his pipe a moment.*) Walt, since that revenoor is come in these parts, I don't like fer yer ol' man to send in the watchers like he allus does afore we git the run off.

WALT

Oh, well, but I don't reckon thar's any danger. He's been at it fer 'bout forty year an' hain't got took yit. I'll say sumpin' to him about it afore long.

MOSE

Ye'd better not to-night. Th' ol' man's mad as a hornet to-night. Ever'thing's gone wrong an' he's a-bilin' over.

WALT

Ye needn't worry. I know th' ol' man better'n that. (*There is a sound of heavy footsteps outside as* NOAH *stumbles in the thicket and mutters an oath.*) That's him comin' now. Don't ye say a word 'bout Mary's bein' here, hear?

MOSE

Yeah, but some o' these nights he's goin' t' send in his watchers too early fer th' last time.

WALT

Don't reckon so, but if'n he does—then au re-war!

(*The sound of tramping draws nearer and*

NOAH *stamps heavily in. He is a stocky mountaineer, sixty-five years of age—heavy-set, active and muscular. He wears dirty breeches, stained with mash, rough laced boots, a worn hunter's coat and blue shirt. His bushy gray hair sticks through the torn crown of the old hat which he wears jammed down on his head. His face is covered with a stubby gray beard. He looks crabbed and sullen.*

SANK *snores on.* MOSE *smokes in silence. As* NOAH *enters,* WALT *stirs the mash industriously, but he stops and leans lazily on his paddle as the old man goes to the still and begins fussing with the fire, muttering to himself.* NOAH *glares at him several times, then bursts out.*)

NOAH

Walt, durn yer lazy hide! Stir that mash an' git a move on ye.

WALT

Oui, oui, mess-sure. But, pa, what ye want t' rush so fer? I'll git this mash ready toot-sweet, 'fore ye're ready fer it.

NOAH

Stop yer durn toot-sweetin' an' git t' work. How the devil d'ye 'spect to git this run done 'fore mornin' if ye ain't a-goin' to work!

(NOAH *continues to work at the still.* WALT *stirs the mash for a few moments and then leans idly on his paddle once more.*

MOSE

(*Still sprawling on the ground*)

T'other night, like I was a-tellin' ye, Walt, when I was comin' back from takin' that run o' brandy down to Lenore, I heared that man Abner had been kind o' hangin' roun' yer sis Mary.

WALT

Who tol' ye that? (*He pokes his mash paddle at* SANK'S *nose.*) Wake up thar, Sank! Fall out!

(WALT *laughs.* SANK *sleepily strikes at the paddle and begins to yawn and stretch.*)

MOSE

I heared it down to Patterson when I was a-comin' back, but I disrecollec' who tol' it.

WALT

Pertite madamerzelle! D'ye hear that, pa?

(NOAH *works on, sullenly refusing to answer.* SANK *is now sufficiently awake to catch the last remark.*)

SANK

Hear what, Walt? Hear what, ye say?

MOSE

Hear that Mary's been a-carryin' on with that Abner. Ye hyeard it.

SANK

Yes, Walt, that's right, so 'tis, so 'tis. I heared Jinkins, the Post Office man, down to Patterson say, says he, that this here Abner was a revenooer fer he got letters from the givermint, so he did—an' that he's a-carryin' on with Mary, so he was.

NOAH

(*Unable to remain silent any longer, turns and glares at* SANK)

That's a ding-busted lie!

WALT

No, 'tain't, pa. I seed Mary talkin' to 'im.

NOAH

Then why in hell didn't ye . . .

WALT

'Twon't do, pa. I thought about it, but I larned when they took me to camp that it was beaucoo hell to pay fer gittin' one o' his kind. Then over thar in France one time . . .

NOAH

Dad-durn France! Hit don't make a dang what ye larned in France. Hit's a-goin' down the Ridge thar that this here Abner is a revenooer.

WALT

Parlay voo! How'd ye git like that, pa? (NOAH *again turns to his work in surly silence.*) Say, pa, air ye sure o' that? (NOAH *refuses to answer and* WALT *points to him, laughing.*) That mess-sure no parlay Fransay.

(*He picks up a can of liquor near him and*

drinks from it, then offers it to MOSE *and* SANK. *Both refuse.*)

MOSE

Too early in the mornin' to drink. Want my liquor in the daytime or in the fore part o' the night. 'Bout time Bill was comin' fer his liquor.

SANK

Yes, it be, an' it be. He ought to soon be here.

MOSE

Bill's ol' 'oman said that Mary was purty well took with that Abner feller.

SANK

She must be, yes she be. My ol' 'oman said that Bill's ol' 'oman said that Mary sees a right smart o' that feller.

WALT

How d'ye know Mary sees 'im?

MOSE

I heared said that Mary meets him in the day time while ye're sleepin', Noah.

SANK

Yes, she do, an' she do.

WALT

Pa, d'ye hear that?

NOAH

(*Unable to hold in any longer, now bursts out in a rage*)

Dod gast her divilish soul, a gal o' mine carryin' on with a revenooer! She ain't been the same since she came back from that thar ding-busted school over thar to Boone. Dod-burn her durned hide! I's allus agin' her goin' over thar, but her ma sent her, an' then layed down an' died on me, an' left her fer me to ten' to.

WALT

You ain't tended to her, much, pa. Ye been tendin' to this here most o' yer time.

NOAH

(*Furiously*)

Who in hell axed ye to speak? Stir that mash, damn ye, stir that mash. (WALT *goes to work as* NOAH *fumes on.*) So ye think I'd let a gal o' mine marry one o' them danged revenooers, do ye?

WALT

No, pa, but . . .

NOAH

Shet up, durn ye, shet up! (*Stamping about in a rage.*) I'd see her in hell first! I'd . . .

SANK

That's right, Noah. So 'tis, so 'tis. I don't blame ye, so I don't, so I . . .

NOAH

(*Turning on him*)

Shet up! Who axed ye t' speak?

SANK

(*Fawningly*)

Well, Noah, I . . .

NOAH

Shet up, I said. What're ye doin' here anyhow?

SANK

Ye tol' us to come an' git this run o' liquor to take to Patterson, so ye did.

NOAH

How ye goin' to 'spect me to git this run off an' ye an' Mose settin' aroun' runnin' yer mouths. Git that thar bucket an' go fotch some water. If'n I's as ding-busted lazy as the rest o' ye, I never would git 'nough juice made fer them thar judges an' lawyers, not to say nothin' 'bout them preachers.

(MOSE *and* SANK *hurry off with a bucket.* NOAH *continues to fume around the still.*)

WALT

Pa, 'tother day when we's a-talkin' 'bout that thar man, Abner, bein' a revenooer, Mary comes in an' says that he wa'n't no revenooer, an' that he's some kind o' magerzine scribbler, or somethin', an' we axed 'er how she knowed it, an' she said she jes' knowed he wa'n't.

(NOAH *pays no attention to him.* MOSE *and* SANK *enter with the water.*)

SANK

Yeah, that's so, so 'tis, fer Mary tol' my ol' 'oman that you all was tellin' lies 'bout that thar man Abner, she did, so she did. An' she said that Abner's a better man than any of us 'uns, she did, so she did . . .

NOAH

(*Breaking out*)

Consarn ye! Bring that thar water here. (*He grabs the bucket.*) What ye standin' thar fer? (*He goes to pour the water into the still, but in his anger he spills it on the fire, almost putting it out. He turns on* SANK *furiously.*) Dod-limb ye, Sank! Dod gast ye, ye goozle-necked ol' fool ye! What ye a-goin' an' puttin' that thar fire out fer? Ding-bust ye, yer . . .

SANK

(*Cringing*)

I didn't put it out, Noah, so I . . .

NOAH

(*Sputtering*)

Ye . . . ye . . . ye hum-duzzled . . .

SANK

(*Shrinking from him*)

Leastwise I didn't go fer to do it, Noah, so I didn't.

WALT

Pa, ye put the fire out yerself, an'—

NOAH

Shet up, ye whing-duzzled yaller boomer ye! Ye ain't no better'n yer sis! Both o' ye be a bunch o' cowards, an' ye . . .

WALT

Oo la-la! Sweet pa-pa!

NOAH

Dod gast ye! Stop that thar la-la-in' an' pa-pa-in' or I'll wring yer neck!

WALT

Aw, pa, I didn't go fer to—

NOAH

Shet up them jaws o' yer'n! D'ye hear me?

MOSE

Noah, my ol' 'oman said that that thar gal o' yer'n went plum' down to the rock to meet that thar Abner, an'—

NOAH

Ding-dang her! I'm a-goin' home right now an' see if'n she'll . . .

(*He starts off right just as three owl hoots ring out in the distance, followed by a shrill "Bob-white."* NOAH *hesitates a moment.*)

MOSE

Thar comes Bill fer his brandy. That's his call. I'll give him the come-on.

(*He returns the call.*)

BILL

(*Singing drunkenly as he approaches from the left*)

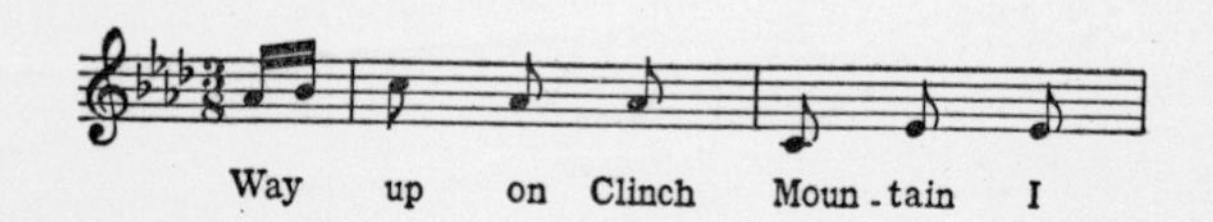

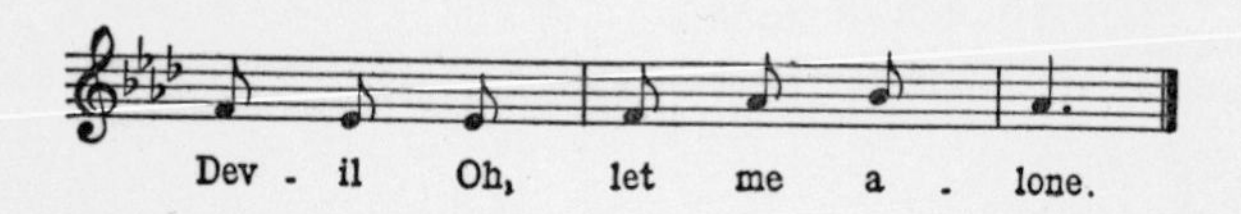

I'll eat when I'm hungry,
  En drink when I'm dry;
En if whiskey don't kill me,
  I'll live till I die.

O Lulu, O Lulu!
  O Lulu, my dear!
I'd give this whole world
  Ef my Lulu was hyer.

Jack o' diamonds, jack o' diamonds,
  I know you of ol'—
You rob my pore pockets
  O' silver an' gol'.

SANK

Ah-hah. Drunk agin'!

BILL

(*He enters from the left.* BILL SPIVINS *is a rough, careless mountaineer. He wears clothes of the same drab tone as those of the other men. His big, bloated face marks him as a heavy drinker and he shows in his singing and in his speech the effects of his liquor. He calls after* NOAH.)

Hey, thar, Noah . . . whar be ye a-goin'? . . . I wanna git my brandy afore ye leave . . . Ye done an' sint yer watchers in, ain't ye? Whar be ye a-goin'? . . .

NOAH

(*Coming back*)

That dod-gasted gal o' mine's been carryin' on with that thar damned revenooer, Abner, an' I jes' started to give her hell, an' make her stop it. A gal o' mine carryin' on with a revenooer!

BILL

Hit must be so then . . . I been down the Ridge . . . an' when I come back my ol' 'oman said that yer gal, Mary . . . was a-carryin' on with him . . .

WALT

What else did she say, Bill? Mary allus tells yer ol' 'oman ever'thing.

BILL

Wal, she said that Mary said that . . . this here Abner wa'n't no revenooer . . . an' that she had met him over thar to Boone . . .

NOAH

She's a-lyin'! That Abner gits letters from the givermint.

SANK

An' he ain't never been to Boone. He's a furriner in these parts, an' he's a ding-busted revenooer.

BILL

My ol' 'oman says Mary wants to run off with him . . . but she's skeered to, fer she knows what ye'd do, Noah. . . . An' she says he ain't no revenooer an' she's goin' t' show us he ain't . . . an' that she's a-goin' t' marry him.

NOAH

Dod gast her! I'll be the one to say about that. My gal run off with a revenooer! No, by the holy damn, I'll see her in hell first!

BILL

My ol' 'oman said that Mary was jes' like her ma . . . an' that she's up to somethin' now . . . an' if'n ye didn't watch out she'd marry that revenooer yit.

SANK

Yes, she will, Noah, so she will. Ye'd better watch her, so ye had.

NOAH

Shet up, Sank, ye ding-busted ol' jay-hawk ye, shet up!

BILL

My ol' 'oman said . . . that yer ol' 'oman allus had her way 'fore she died . . . an' that she didn't listen to ye when she didn't want . . .

NOAH

Dod gast yer ol' 'oman! She's allus sayin' too much. Gimme yer jug. (*He takes the jug, fills it, and hands it back to* BILL.) Don't ye fergit to bring me them 'taters to pay fer this. Ye owe me two bushels now.

BILL

My ol' 'oman said that that man Abner's up in these parts to-day . . . an' thet yer gal met him over to the rock, an' that she believed they's up to somethin'! Mary ain't been home to-day. . . . Ye'd better watch her, Noah. . . . She'll git ye yit.

NOAH

Dad burn ye, git out o' here! A gal o' mine an' a revenooer git me! Ye ding-busted yaller-livered fool, git out! Ain't I the best man on this side o' the Ridge? Ain't I boss here?

SANK

Yes, ye be, Noah, so ye be.

(BILL *reels out with his jug.*)

MOSE

Noah, 'tother night down to Curtis's store I heared that Abner was sent here by the givermint to git ye fer killin' that other revenooer a few years ago.

NOAH

(*Startled*)

What's that? What're ye sayin', Mose? Ye're a liar! That's what ye are. Ye're a liar, I say! Ye're . . .

MOSE

Stop that, Noah. I's givin' ye straight talk, an' ye ain't to be callin' me a liar. I don't have to work fer ye, an' I ain't a-goin' to. . . .

NOAH

(*More calmly*)

I didn't mean it 'zactly like that, Mose, but . . . but . . .

MOSE

That's the truth, Noah. Ol' man Jinkins tol' hit hisself.

SANK

Yes it be, so it be. I heared him myself, so I did.

WALT

Pa, that's why he's been hangin' roun' Mary. He's tryin' to pick it out o' her, so he c'n git us, an' he's caught her. That's hit.

(*At this moment* MARY SETZER *carefully peers through the rhododendron branches at the right. She is a pretty mountain girl, simply dressed in a plain but becoming pink gingham. Without having been seen, she withdraws noiselessly into the bushes again.*)

NOAH

Gol ding her, she ain't got no more sense 'n to let him ketch her an' then let him be hangin' 'roun to spy an' larn all he can.

WALT

Pa, hadn't we better skip an' git out'n this?

NOAH

An' leave all this an' be skeered to come back to git it? No, I ain't goin' t' let no revenooer run me. They ain't never done it yit an' they ain't never goin' t' do hit. I'll go down thar to Patterson to-morrow, an' I'll take ol' Beck over thar (*pointing to his rifle*), an' I'll fix this here dod-gasted, ding-fuzzled revenooer like I did 'tother'n. An' then I'll take that gal o' mine . . .

(NOAH *is interrupted by* LAURENCE ABNER, *who breaks through the thicket at the right, followed by* MARY SETZER, *who keeps a safe distance in the rear, yet is on the alert, ready to assist him if necessary.* ABNER *is a good-looking young man, trimly dressed in clothes suitable for mountain wear.*)

ABNER

(*Firing a shot and then covering the moonshiners with a pistol*)

Hands up, gents! (*They turn, startled.* WALT *and* MOSE *spring toward the rifles but* ABNER *stops them.*) None of that, gents. It'll mean death if you try it again.

NOAH

Dod gast ye!

ABNER

First time a revenuer ever had the ups on you, isn't it? Now, gents, kindly move over to this side and remove your coats so that I may see that you are not armed. (*The men obey his orders as he motions them over to the left with his pistols.*) No tricks, remember! I learned to shoot pretty straight in the army.

WALT

Larned to shoot in the army, huh? Wal, that hain't nothin'. While I 's over thar in France I captured 'bout forty Bochers, three big rumble-bumble guns, an' a dozen or more rifles an' . . .

MARY

(*Advancing*)

Aw, now, Walt, ye wa'n't never up at the shootin' line. Ye said ye peeled 'taters all the time.

WALT

Parlay whippay dally doodle doo! Air *ye* here, Sis? Wal, ye jes' watch the ol' man.

NOAH

(*Seeing* MARY)

Dod gast ye, gal! Ding-damn ye! Here's that damned ol' jay-pipin' horn frog what ye been a-hangin' aroun' with—ye see now if he ain't a revenooer, don't ye? Dad-burn yer hum-duzzled soul! Consarn the dod-limbed hide o' ye! Ye see whar yer pa is, do ye? Damn ye, I'll fix ye. . . .

(*He starts toward* MARY, *but* ABNER *motions him back with his pistol.*)

ABNER

Hold on there! You want to be careful and not forget that I've got you at present, and the law doesn't deal any too lightly with your kind, especially since prohibition.

(WALT *slinks around behind the mash tub and picks up a club. The "revenooer" is occupied watching* NOAH, *and* WALT *steals closer to him, while the old man rages.*)

NOAH

Damn ye, ye yaller-back 'tater bug ye! Ye got me now, but ye jes' wait. What ye goin' t' do with us?

ABNER

What would you give me to let you off?

NOAH

(*Surprised*)

What! What's that ye say?

(WALT *has now crept up close behind* ABNER. *He raises his club and springs forward, but* MARY *seizes his arm.*)

MARY

Don't try nothin' like that, Walt. Hit won't work.

NOAH

(*Regaining his voice, he sputters in his uncontrolled rage*)

Ding-damn ye! Dod gast ye . . . ye . . . ye . . . consarn ye . . . ye . . . damn ye . . . ye be helping this here revenooer to take yer own pa. So that's what ye come here fer, ye durn yaller boomer ye! Ye divilish dog! Ye allus was jes' like yer ma. Ye said he wa'n't no revenooer, so ye did. Well, ye lied, gal, ye lied, an' I'll git ye. . . .

ABNER

Hold on a minute. You seem to forget that I've got you all just at present, and I'm likely to keep you. But just for the fun of knowing—what would you give me to let you go?

NOAH

Ding-bust ye! By that rotten mash over thar . . .

ABNER

Don't swear by the mash, I've captured it, too.

SANK

So he has, Noah, so he has.

NOAH

Dad durn ye, Sank! Damn ye—Walt—if ye'd do somethin'—if ye'd drag him off—he wouldn't be standin' there with his gun drawed on us. But ye stand thar a-runnin' yer clop-trop mouths an' doin' nothin'. Why don't ye . . .

WALT

Holy scents of sweet smellin' asserfiditty! Why don't ye do hit yerself, pa?

ABNER

Here now, let's come to business. If you're not going to make me an offer, I'll make you one. If you'll let me marry your daughter, we'll call this off. What do you say?

NOAH

(*Amazed*)

What's that? (*Beginning to understand, he stamps the ground in a rage and advances toward* ABNER, *who motions him back with his pistols.*) Marry my gal, a revenooer marry my gal! Ye dod gasted pole-cat ye! Ye ding-busted stinkin' possum skunk! Ye bow-legged 'tater-bug ye! I'll see ye in Heck's ol' pine field twenty miles 'tother side o' hell first. I'll . . . I'll . . .

ABNER

Just a minute before you go on. Listen to this—if I take you down the Ridge, as I certainly will if you don't do as I say, think of the days in prison. You're an old man and you would probably die there between the walls, behind the bars. People would come to see you, and point their fingers through the bars at you as they do the animals at the circus, and they'd say, "There's Noah Setzer. He used to be the leader on this side of the ridge, but a revenuer gets them all, and one got him." Then there'll be your son and all these other fellows in cages beside you. . . .

SANK

That's right, Noah, so 'tis, so 'tis. He'll take us all, so he will, an' . . .

NOAH

Shet up, ye . . .

ABNER

And then there's another thing I want to tell you before I take you. I have the proof that you and your son were the men who killed the revenue officers four years ago. At your trial I shall turn the evidence against you both. That means death for you.

NOAH

Wh-wh-what's that . . .

ABNER

Just think! They'll lead you, the boss of the Ridge, in like a cow, and sit you down in a chair. And then they'll turn on just enough juice to burn you, and let you know how it feels. Then gradually they'll turn it on full force and your bones will snap and it'll cook the flesh off your live body!

SANK

Give him yer gal, Noah, give him yer gal!

MARY

(*Glancing at* ABNER *with a smile*)

Pa, he's got ye, so ye'd better give in. If ye don't, jes' think what the Ridge'll say when he takes ye to jail. Ye'll be the only Setzer they've ever got yet! I'm willin' to marry him, an' if you'll let me, it'll save us all. I'm goin' t' marry him, anyhow.

NOAH

Well, marry him an' . . . damn ye both!

ABNER

(*Lowering his pistol, and laughing*)

Thank you, Mr. Setzer.

NOAH

Damn ye . . . don't "Mister" me! An' I don't want none o' yer thanks. . . . (*To* MARY *and* ABNER, *who are now both convulsed with laughter.*) What're ye laughin' at?

ABNER

Well, you see I'm not a revenue officer after all. I'm just a magazine writer up in these mountains collecting materials and—incidentally (*Smiling at* MARY)—a wife. This has been the first real fun I've had since the Boston Police Riot.

NOAH

Ye're not a . . . a . . . dod gasted . . .

MARY

(*Who has been standing by* ABNER'S *side, now steps forward*)

No, he ain't, pa. We wanted to git married, but I couldn't think of runnin' away like Laurence wanted me to, an' the whole Ridge a-thinkin' that me, a Setzer, had run away with a revenooer. An' then, I couldn't a never come back, fer ye'd 'a got us.

SANK

Yes, he would-'a, so he would-'a.

Scene from *Dod Gast Ye Both!* a comedy of mountain moonshiners, by Hubert Heffner. LAWRENCE ABNER (George Crawford); MARY (Ione Markham); NOAH SETZER, her father (George Denny); WALT, his son (Wilbur Stout); SINK (Hubert Heffner, the author); MOSE (Chester Burton). The still used is a genuine 80-gallon copper still captured by "revenooers" from a band of Orange County moonshiners.

NOAH: Here, take this here quart and clear out o' here an' stay out an' . . . . an' . . . . . **dod gast ye both!**

MARY

An' we wanted to be married right away, but we couldn't think o' no way to prove that Laurence wa'n't no revenooer, so we—

ABNER

(*Breaking in*)

Mary happened to remember a hold-up like this which she told me about when we were over at Boone, and then—

WALT

(*Interrupting, with a loud guffaw*)

And then ye planned all this jes' to git us?

(MARY *and* ABNER *nod a smiling assent.*)

ABNER

Yes, and I'm going to get a corking good story out of it, too.

WALT

Pa, ye said a revenooer wa'n't never goin' t' git ye! Why he ain't even a revenooer's picter an' he's got ye!

NOAH

(*Unable to restrain his rage*)

Dad burn ye! Ding dang ye, . . . an' ye hain't no revenooer . . . ! If I'd a knowed that . . . dad burn ye . . . by jumpin' Jupiter's horn snake, I'll not stand fer hit. . . . I'll . . .

MARY

Hold on, thar, pa, ye've done give yer promise, an' Walt an' Mose an' Sank all heared ye.

SANK

Yes, ye did, Noah, an' ye did!

MARY

We got ye, pa, an' ye can't go back on yer promise. So we're goin' to git married an' stay on right here.

NOAH

(*Violently*)

Damn ye! Dod-limb ye . . . ye hum-duzzled . . . (*He recovers his composure, takes a quart bottle, goes to the still and fills it from the worm.*) I'll git even wid ye. Jes' wait, I'll git ye, durn ye! (*He hands the bottle to* ABNER.) Here, take this here quart, an' clear out o' here, an' stay out, an—(*He stands, shaking his fists at them as they go off laughing. There is just the trace of a grin on his face*)—an' dod-gast ye both!

CURTAIN

OFF NAGS HEAD[1]
OR THE BELL BUOY

A Tragedy of the North Carolina Coast

BY

DOUGALD MACMILLAN

1 Copyright, 1922, by The Carolina Playmakers, Inc. Permission to produce this play may be secured by addressing Frederick H. Koch, Director, The Carolina Playmakers, Inc., Chapel Hill, North Carolina.

OFF NAGS HEAD
OR THE BELL BUOY

CAST OF CHARACTERS

As originally produced at The Play-House, Chapel Hill, North Carolina, April 30 and May 1, 1920.

AN OLD FISHERMAN,	Jonathan Daniels
THE "GAL," *his daughter,*	Mildred Sherrill
THE SICK WOMAN, *the fisherman's wife,*	Aline Hughes
THE DOCTOR,	David Reid Hodgin
THE OLD WOMAN,	Elizabeth Taylor

SCENE: A fisherman's hut on the sand dunes of Nags Head on the North Carolina Coast.

TIME: September, 1869. A stormy night.

OFF NAGS HEAD

SCENE

A Fisherman's *hut on the North Carolina sand banks, at Nags Head.*

The roar of the surf and the distant clanging of the bell buoy can be heard before the curtain rises on a room furnished meagrely and not very neat in appearance. There is a door at the back to the left, opening out on the beach; to the right a small window, closed by a rough shutter. Between the door and the window, on the back wall, hangs an old portrait in a tarnished gilded frame. It is a handsome painting of a young woman. At the beginning of the play it is covered by a coarse woolen cloth.

There is a fireplace in the left side wall and in that corner a table with a water bucket. On the right a door opens into the adjoining room. A lantern, hung on a nail by the fireplace, gives a flickering light.

It is nearly dark on an evening in September and a storm is piling up mountains of spray in the surf, some distance across the beach. Throughout the entire action the roar of the surf and the ringing of the bell buoy can be heard. It is far away, but you could hear it at any time; only, when some one is talking, you do not notice the distant clanging. From time to time the wind howls around the house, and every now and then the smoke blows out of the fireplace, in which a fire of driftwood is struggling to overcome the draft down the chimney.

A woman is lying on a low bed in the corner of the room to the right. She is moaning as if she were suffering acutely. The old FISHERMAN *is standing by the bed with a conch-shell of water in his hand. He touches the woman on the shoulder.*

FISHERMAN

Here, want a drink o' water?

(*The woman moans and raises her head slightly. The* FISHERMAN *holds the shell to her lips. She drinks a swallow and sinks back on the bed. The* FISHERMAN *puts the shell on top of the water bucket and, crossing to the fireplace, begins to mend a shrimp seine lying across a chair. He sits down with the seine in his lap. The* SICK WOMAN *moans again and moves restlessly. He turns toward her.*)

Doctor Wright'll be here purty soon. The gal's been gone long enough to be back.

(*After a moment of silence the door at the back opens and the* GIRL *comes in with an apron full of driftwood that she has picked up on the beach. She has a shawl drawn tightly around her shoulders and her colorless hair has been blown into wisps about her freckled face. She whines in a nasal drawl when she talks. Dragging her heels, she shuffles over to the fireplace and drops the wood in a pile on the hearth.*

The FISHERMAN *turns to the door as she comes in, speaking anxiously.*)

Is he comin'?

GIRL

Doctor Wright's gone over to Jug Neck an' won't be back till to-morrow. I foun' a docto' at ol' man Stokes's though. He come thar to-day from Raleigh. He's comin'. (*She hangs her shawl on a hook behind the door and goes to the* SICK WOMAN.) Is it bad?

(*The* SICK WOMAN *groans.*)

FISHERMAN

Did you see the ol' 'oman?

GIRL

Naw. Is she gone?

FISHERMAN

Been gone 'bout an hour.

GIRL

Which way'd she go?

FISHERMAN

Toward the inlet.

GIRL

(*She rises from bending over the* SICK WOMAN *and goes to the door for her shawl.*)

M . . . hm. Time she was back. I'll go hunt 'er.

FISHERMAN

Wait. Maybe she'll come in in a minute. I'll go hunt. How high is the tide now?

GIRL

(*Hangs up her shawl again but speaks anxiously*)
Them stakes fo' Jones's shack is covered an' it's washin' up under the seine racks.

FISHERMAN

M . . . hm. Purty bad.

GIRL

An' it's so misty you can't see the Topsail Light.

(*She goes to the fireplace and crouches there, warming her hands.*)

FISHERMAN

Huh. This is a worse storm'n we've had in a long time.

(*He goes to the door and looks out. The bell buoy clangs.*)

GIRL

Listen to that bell buoy. It makes me feel so quar.

(*She shivers.*)

FISHERMAN

Don' you take on like that. The ol' 'oman's bad enough.

GIRL

(*She takes an old, round, iron kettle and fills it with water from the bucket by the door*)

She's been bad all day—like she was las' storm we had when she tried to jump off'n the landin'! She might try again. We better look for 'er.

(*She hangs the kettle over the fire and crosses to the* SICK WOMAN.)

FISHERMAN

I reckon so. You look out for yo' ma.

GIRL

The ol' 'oman's been a-doin' like she done that day when she tried to run in the surf with the picter.

FISHERMAN

Has she? (*As though he doesn't quite understand why.*) She sets a lot o' store by that picter.

GIRL

I'm kind o' skeered she'll do somethin' bad some day.

FISHERMAN

She ain't gonna jump in the surf no more. Not on a col' night like this un. You take care o' yo' ma thar. I'll hunt th' other un. (*He starts toward the door and opens it. The* OLD WOMAN *is seen outside just coming in. She has been tall and might have been imperious. She speaks with a more refined accent than the others. She is demented and they humor her. The* FISHERMAN *speaks to her from the doorway.*) Well, we was jest a-comin' to look fo' you! Thought you might 'a fallen overboard or sumpthin'.

(*He sits down again by the fire. The* GIRL *takes the* OLD WOMAN'S *shawl from her shoulders and hangs it by the fireplace to dry. The* OLD WOMAN *does not seem to notice the others but speaks as though to herself.*)

OLD WOMAN

I've had so much to do.

FISHERMAN

Well, now that's bad. You mustn't work too hard. It's bad for you.

OLD WOMAN

It's better to work than to think. (*She smiles in a vague sort of way. Her eyes are expressionless.*) There are times when I think and I hear things. They keep calling me on the boat and the bell buoy rings——

GIRL

(*To the* FISHERMAN)

Ain't it time the doctor was comin'?

OLD WOMAN

I see many things. There is the cheery crowd on the boat and they keep calling, for all is dark and everything reels—the light comes close and all is dark again. Listen! my baby boy calls—the water roars and we all get wet. . . . But I still have my work. I must not give up—I still have my child and my pic-

Elizabeth Taylor as THE OLD WOMAN in *Off Nag's Head* or *The Bell Buoy*, a tragedy of the North Carolina Coast, by Dougald MacMillan.

THE OLD WOMAN: There are times when I think and I hear things. They keep calling me on the boat and the bell buoy rings . . . . but I still have my work. I must not give up. I still have my child and my picture to work for.

ture to work for. (*She goes toward the curtained portrait.*) My dead boy and you—(*She pulls the curtain aside, displaying the beautiful old painting. Her voice is more cheerful and less troubled as she speaks to the* FISHERMAN.) It is a picture of me! Don't you think it is good? It was done by the best artist. I am taking it to my father in New York.

FISHERMAN
(*Humoring her*)

Yes, yes. You done tol' us that a lot o' times.

GIRL
(*To the* FISHERMAN)

I wonder why the doctor ain't come.

OLD WOMAN
(*Interrupting and still speaking to the* FISHERMAN)

So I have—so I have. Well, I must keep on working. I've had a message from my father. (*More brightly.*) I'm going to leave soon. (*She starts toward the room at the right, then turns to the* FISHERMAN, *speaking anxiously.*) Take care of her. Don't let anyone get her. (*Speaking to the portrait.*) I am going to take you with me when I go to New York to see my father. (*She goes out, glancing back from the door at the portrait.*) I'm coming back soon.

FISHERMAN

She's so scared someun's gonna steal her picter. . . . Is the lamp lit in thar?

GIRL

Yeah. I lit it. (*There is a knock on the door.*) It must be the new doctor.

(*She opens the door and the* DOCTOR *comes in. He is an elderly man, wearing a long cloak and carrying a satchel. His manner is brisk and cheerful and he is rather talkative, the old family doctor type.*

FISHERMAN

Come in.

DOCTOR

Thank you. I had some trouble finding the house. There is so much mist you can't see very well. I believe this is the worst storm I ever saw.

FISHERMAN

Yeah. It's bad. You can't even see the Topsail Light.

DOCTOR

(*Taking off his hat and cloak and laying them on a chair by the fire*)

Do you often have storms like this one? This is my first trip down here. Mr. Stokes asked me down to go fishing with him.

FISHERMAN

This un is right bad.

DOCTOR

Now, where is the sick woman?

FISHERMAN
(Pointing to the bed)

Here.

DOCTOR

Oh, yes! Your wife?

FISHERMAN

Yes, suh.

DOCTOR
(Sitting by the bed)

How do you feel?

(The SICK WOMAN *moans.)*

FISHERMAN

She don' say nothin'. She's got a misery in her chist.

DOCTOR

I see. How long has she been this way?

FISHERMAN

Since this mornin'.

DOCTOR
(To the GIRL, *who stands by the door to the next room)*

Will you bring me some water, please.

(She goes out. He opens his satchel and takes out a bottle, pouring some medicine into the cup which the GIRL *brings him, and gives it to the sick woman to drink. The* FISHERMAN *and*

the GIRL *look on in silence. He speaks reassuringly.)*

She'll be comfortable in a few minutes. It is not serious this time, but she must not work too hard.

(He rises and crosses to the fireplace for his cloak.)

FISHERMAN

Will you set down an' rest yourself an' git dry? It's a long walk back to Stokes's.

DOCTOR

Why, thank you, I believe I will.

(They sit before the fire and light their pipes. The GIRL *goes out.)*

FISHERMAN

You ain't been here befo', Doctor?

DOCTOR

No. This is my first trip. I've always wanted to come but never had a chance before. There are lots of interestin' tales told about your beaches and islands around here.

FISHERMAN

Yeah. I reckon thar's a lot o' tales.

DOCTOR

Captain Kidd is said to have buried money on every island on the coast.

FISHERMAN

Yes, suh. Right over thar on Haw's Hammock my pa dug up a chist.

DOCTOR

Was there anything in it?

FISHERMAN

No.

(*He smiles.*)

DOCTOR

That's often the way. (*He laughs, then stops to listen to the wind, which is increasing in volume and intensity.*) Listen to that! This would be a good night for the land pirates that used to be around here. Did you know any of them?

FISHERMAN

I don' know what you mean.

DOCTOR

Oh, is that so? Why, they say there used to be a band of men around here that hung lights on a horse's head and drove the horse down the beach. From a distance it looked like a ship. Ships at sea were often fooled by it and ran aground. When they did, the men on shore plundered them and killed the crew. That's how Nags Head got its name.

FISHERMAN

(*Showing some confusion*)

Is that right?

DOCTOR

Why, you are old enough to know about that. I'm surprised that you didn't know some of those old rascals.

FISHERMAN

(*Turning away*)

We don't talk much in these parts.

DOCTOR

(*Becoming interested in his tale*)

A very famous case, I remember—one that has been talked about for a long time. I heard it from my mother, was that of a boat named the . . . *The Patriot*. She was bound for New York from Georgetown, I believe. An illustrious lady, Theodosia Burr, was on board—the daughter of Aaron Burr. The boat disappeared somewhere along this coast. That was about fifty years ago, and none of the crew has been heard of since. (*The* FISHERMAN *is silent, looking into the fire. The* DOCTOR *rises.*) Well, let's have another look at the patient. I'll have to get back pretty soon. Stokes gets me out early these days to get the blue fish on the right time o' the tide.

(*He knocks out his pipe against the chimney and turns toward the bed. The* FISHERMAN *rises. The* OLD WOMAN *enters unnoticed, crosses to the fireplace and stands there watching the others. The* DOCTOR *starts to the bed but stops suddenly, astonished. He has seen the portrait!*)

Why, hello, what's that?

FISHERMAN

What?

DOCTOR

The portrait. Where did it come from?

FISHERMAN

Oh, we found it on a derelict that drifted in one day.

DOCTOR

(*Becoming excited*)

Why that looks like the picture that was on *The Patriot*. I remember distinctly, I once saw a copy of the lost portrait. It must be the portrait of Theodosia Burr!

(*The* OLD WOMAN *watches them intently.*)

FISHERMAN

Who's she?

DOCTOR

The woman that was lost. Where were the crew and passengers on the boat?

FISHERMAN

I don' recollect no people on 'er. I reckon thar wan't no people on 'er.

DOCTOR

Where were they?

FISHERMAN

I don' know.

DOCTOR

Was the boat named *The Patriot?*

FISHERMAN

I can't say, 'cause I don' exactly know. She might 'a been *The Patriot* or she might 'a been the *Mary Ann*—I can't say.

(*He has become sullen.*)

DOCTOR

Come, now. Tell me about it.

FISHERMAN

I don' know no more. We jest found it.

(*He turns away.*)

DOCTOR

Then I must have the portrait. I'm sure it's the key to the Theodosia Burr mystery. Will you sell it?

(*The* OLD WOMAN *watches him, frightened.*)

FISHERMAN

(*Looking at her*)

I dunno as how we would. We sets a lot o' store by that picter.

DOCTOR

I'll pay you for it. How much do you want?

(*He starts to take the picture from the wall. The* OLD WOMAN, *who has been moving toward it, seizes his arm, excitedly.*)

OLD WOMAN

Sell her! Sell my picture! She is one of the things I work for—my dead boy and my picture. You shall not take them from me. (*She lifts the portrait from its place and holds it tightly in her arms, talking to it.*) I am taking you to my father in New York. He wants it. (*More wildly, speaking to the* DOCTOR.) You shan't have it. . . . They shan't take you from me. . . . It is all that I have. I've been cruelly treated. My baby boy died. He is out there. . . . (*She points to the sea.*) He often calls me to come to him but I must stay here, for I still have my picture to work for.

(*She turns away.*)

DOCTOR

Who are you?

OLD WOMAN

(*Smiling. She seems to look at something far away*) Ah. . . .

DOCTOR

Who are you? What do you know about the picture? It must be a portrait of Theodosia Burr!

OLD WOMAN

Burr? Theodosia Burr? (*Almost frenzied as she suddenly remembers her identity.*) Why, she's the person that I stand for! I've been thinking—she keeps talking to me. That's who I stand for!

DOCTOR

What?

FISHERMAN

(*With a significant nod*)

Don' mind her. She ain't right.

OLD WOMAN

I must be going now. They are tired of waiting. I've stayed here long enough. . . . I'm coming, father.

(*She starts to go into the next room.*)

DOCTOR

(*Stepping in front of the door, he speaks gently*) Where are you going?

OLD WOMAN

(*Turning back into the room*)

Maybe the boat's fixed now. I wonder where the others are.

DOCTOR

(*Persuasively*)

Yes, tell us where the others are.

OLD WOMAN

Oh, I remember. They're gone. They were killed. Hush, don't you hear them . . . listen! . . . *They* took all the things on the boat, but I have saved you. (*She clasps the picture closer and stares before her.*) It was an awful storm like this one. A false light, we ran on the beach. It was horrible! Yes . . . yes, *they* were there—*they,* they killed them all!

DOCTOR

Yes, yes! Don't get excited. We'll fix everything all right. Don't let it worry you. Sit down and tell us all about it.

OLD WOMAN

(*Moving to the right of the room*)

I am going away very soon now. . . . I saw a sign to-day. I have been sent for. They have sent for me to come to see my father in New York. He has been waiting so long. I must go——

(*She goes out into the adjoining room, muttering. The* DOCTOR *turns to the* FISHERMAN.)

DOCTOR

What do you know about this?

FISHERMAN

Nothin', I tol' you.

DOCTOR

How did she get here?

FISHERMAN

We took 'er in one time.

(*He speaks sullenly.*)

DOCTOR

Yes, but where did she come from? You know more about this, and you're going to tell me. If you don't, I'll have you arrested on suspicion. You'll be tried and maybe you'll be hanged. Now, tell me what you know.

FISHERMAN

Wait—(*He is beginning to be afraid*)—I don't know nothin', I tol' you.

DOCTOR

(*Threateningly*)

Yes, you do. Do you want to get into court?

FISHERMAN

No! No!

DOCTOR

(*Raising his voice*)

Then tell me what you know about it. I'll——

FISHERMAN

(*Interrupting*)

Be quiet, I'll tell you. Don' make no noise . . . I was a boy . . . they used to hang a lantern on a horse . . . then when the ship run aground they got all the stuff off'n 'er . . .

DOCTOR

Land pirates! I thought you knew! Go on.

FISHERMAN

That's all.

DOCTOR

What became of the people on these boats?

FISHERMAN

They got drownded.

DOCTOR

How? Don't take so long.

FISHERMAN

Jes' drownded.

DOCTOR

Did you kill them?

FISHERMAN

No. They was jes' drownded.

DOCTOR

And where did the old woman and the portrait come from?

FISHERMAN

They was on one o' the boats an' we took 'em in. She ain't been right in 'er head sence. Her baby boy died that night.

DOCTOR

Where did she go? I want to talk to her again.

(*He goes toward the door.*)

FISHERMAN

You ain't a-goin' t'——

DOCTOR

(*Interrupting*)

No, I won't send you to jail. Go get the old woman.

(*He moves to the fireplace.*)

FISHERMAN

She went in thar. (*He goes to the door and looks into the next room.*) She ain't in thar now.

DOCTOR

Then where could she be?

FISHERMAN

I dunno.

(*The* GIRL *comes in, very much excited and frightened. She enters by the door at the back and as she opens it the roar of the surf and the ringing of the bell buoy may be heard more distinctly.*)

GIRL

I tried to stop 'er, but she jest went on! I can't do nothin' with 'er.

DOCTOR

What do you mean?

GIRL

She run out a-huggin' that picter. I couldn't stop 'er. She said she was goin' away!

FISHERMAN

Where did she go?

GIRL

I dunno. She's been so bad all day, a-talkin' 'bout the bell buoy a-ringin' for 'er—(*She goes to the* FISHERMAN.) I'm skeered o' what she'll do!

(*Above the roar of the surf can be heard faintly but clearly, a high-pitched, distant cry.*)

DOCTOR

What's that?

FISHERMAN

I dunno . . .

GIRL

I wonder if it's . . .

(*The* DOCTOR *and* FISHERMAN *go to the door at the back*)

DOCTOR

We'd better go look for her.

FISHERMAN

(*As they run out into the darkness across the beach*) I hope she ain't . . .

(*The* GIRL *stands in the open door watching them. The* SICK WOMAN *moans. The roar of the surf and the ringing of the bell buoy are heard more distinctly. After a moment the* FISHERMAN *comes in, breathless and wild-eyed.*)

FISHERMAN

Gi' me the lantern! She's run in the surf an' it a-bilin'.

GIRL

(*Taking the lighted lantern from a nail by the fireplace*)

She said the bell was a-ringin' for 'er. . . . Is she . . .

FISHERMAN

(*Takes the lantern, pausing a moment in the doorway*)

She's drownded! She done washed ashore!

(*The* FISHERMAN *goes out and the light from his lantern disappears in the night. As the* GIRL *stands in the doorway looking toward the sea, the bell buoy can still be heard above the storm.*)

CURTAIN

THE LAST OF THE LOWRIES[1]

A Play of the Croatan Outlaws of Robeson County, North Carolina.

By

PAUL GREENE

THE LAST OF THE LOWRIES

CAST OF CHARACTERS

As originally produced at The Play-House, Chapel Hill, North Carolina, April 30 and May 1, 1920.

CUMBA LOWRIE, *the aged mother of the Lowries,* Elizabeth Taylor
JANE, *her daughter,* Ruth Penny
MAYNO, *Cumba's daughter-in-law,* Rachel Freeman
HENRY BERRY LOWRIE, *last of the outlaw gang,* Ernest Nieman

SCENE: The rough home of the Lowrie gang in Scuffletown, a swampy region of Robeson County, North Carolina.

TIME: A night in the winter of the year 1874.

SCENE

THE kitchen of the Lowrie home.

The interior is that of a rude dwelling built of rough-hewn timbers. At the right front is a fireplace in which a fire is burning. Pots and pans are hung around the fireplace. A rocking chair is drawn up in front of the fire. At the right rear is a cupboard. At the centre rear a door leads outside. Above it are several fishing poles and a net resting on pegs fitted into the joists. To the rear at the left is a loom with a piece of half-finished cloth in it. A door in the centre of the left wall leads into an adjoining room. To the right of it is a window. At the front on that side is a chest. In the centre of the room is a rough, oblong eating-table and several home-made chairs with cowhide bottoms. A spinning-wheel stands at the front left. On the table is an unlighted candle in a tin holder.

The play opens with MAYNO LOWRIE *spinning at the wheel. She stops, folds her hands aimlessly across her lap, and stares idly into the fire. She is a full-blooded Croatan, about twenty-five years old, of medium height with skin a tan color, almost copper, prominent cheek bones, short flat nose, and black shifty eyes. Her coarse raven hair is wound into a knot at the back of her head. She is dressed in a polka-dot calico. Her shoes are somewhat heavy but comfortable looking. Around her neck she wears a string of shiny glass beads. Several cheap rings adorn her hands.*

For a moment she sits idle, and then begins to spin lazily, at almost every revolution of the wheel stopping to glance at the rear door, then at the door to the left, as if expecting someone to enter. She listens. From afar off comes the lone hoot of an owl. She shakes her head and starts the wheel going again. Then she goes to the fireplace, turns the bread in the spider and with a long-handled spoon stirs the peas in the pot. After this she goes back to her chair at the wheel.

Three knocks are heard at the rear door. MAYNO *hurries to remove the bar.* JANE LOWRIE *enters with a bundle under her arm. She throws the bundle on the table, takes off her bonnet and cape and hangs them on a peg near the door at the left.* MAYNO *goes to the bundle, stares at it half curiously and fearfully.* JANE *comes to the fire without speaking. She is a tall Croatan girl, dressed more plainly than* MAYNO *in a dress of homespun, with no ornaments. Her shoes are covered with mud. She is about twenty years old, with heavy black hair, light tan-colored skin, and regular features. Her face is more open and intelligent than* MAYNO'S. *Her whole figure expresses weariness. She looks anxoiusly at the door of the adjoining room, then turns to* MAYNO.

JANE

Has she asked for me?

MAYNO

Not but once. I tol' her you'd stepped over to

Pate's for a little flour, and she seemed to pearten up at that. Said mebbe they'd be a letter from the boys 'way yander.

(*She smiles scornfully. Still standing at the table, she looks at the package.* CUMBA'S *voice is heard calling from the room at the left.*)

CUMBA

Jane, Jane, is that ye?

JANE

(*Going to the door at the left*)

Yes, muh, I'm jes' back from Pate's with the flour.

CUMBA

All right, honey.

(JANE *goes into the room. Their voices can be heard indistinctly.* MAYNO *looks at the package, reaches and touches it. Then she tears a hole in the paper, peers at it intently and draws away.* JANE *comes back.*)

JANE

Mayno, they're . . . his'n!

MAYNO

Whose? . . . Yes, they must be his'n.

JANE

(*Lighting a candle and placing it on the table*)

Yes, Mayno, they's Steve's all right.

MAYNO

How'd you git 'em, chile?

JANE

I got 'em from the sheriff.

MAYNO

And I thought you were goin' to see Henry Berry 'bout Steve's money and find where they put 'im.

(She opens the package and takes out a coat, a pair of trousers, and a black felt hat. The garments are slashed and stiff with blood.)

JANE

I did—two hours proguing down through the black swamps an' the bramble br'ars, and when I foun' Henry Berry he said them sher'ffs what killed Steve got his money, and as for where they put 'im, nobody knows. (CUMBA *is heard groaning as she turns in her bed.* JANE *lowers her voice.*) And then I went to the sheriff for his clothes. I knowed that some day when she—(*Nodding to the room at the left*)—finds it out she'll be wantin' his clothes, them she made with her own hands like th' others. And the sheriff wouldn't tell me where they buried 'im.

MAYNO

Took his money, did they? That's the way with them white folks. They do all they kin agin' us poor Croatons, 'cause we's jes' injuns, they says—though we knows better.

JANE

They don't hold nothin' agin' us; hit's agin' the boys.

MAYNO

They killed yo' daddy and William and Tom and Steve for being robbers and cut-throats and they robbers and cut-throats theyselves. (*Fiercely.*) And me needing new dresses and the like. But they's one left they won't git, the last an' best of 'em all. The day they lays Henry Berry cold they'll be more of 'em got than has been.

JANE

(*Wearily*)

Hush, Mayno; with your jawing you'd wake the dead. She'll hear you.

MAYNO

(*Throwing down the clothes and coming to the fire*)

Well, why you want to keep pushing trouble from her? What's the good o' it? She'll find it out somehow. She's suffered now 'til you cain't hurt her no more. And ain't I suffered too, with my man dead on me? What call has she got to . . .

JANE

No, we ain't a-goin' to tell her now. She ain't got much longer, and let her keep on b'lieving Steve and Henry Berry's safe in Georgy. No, they ain't no use o' letting her on to it now.

(JANE *sits at the spinning-wheel.*)

MAYNO

(*Vehemently*)

Ain't Henry Berry going to *try* to git them sher'ffs back for killing Steve? If I's a outlaw like him I'd a done paid 'em. And he'll pay 'em, too! He's the best o' the Lowries and he'll 'venge them that's been murdered in cold blood like Steve and the rest.

JANE

No, Mayno, he won't nuther. His time's drawin' nigh. He knows it. They're settin' for him everywhere. They's men watchin' this house to-night. I seen it in his face to-day that he's layin' down. He was wrong from the first. He knows it now.

MAYNO

What's that!

JANE

Yes, he's a-quittin', but if them sheriffs hadn't agged him on ten years ago when he wanted to quit and be quiet he'd a been livin' in peace here to-night. But it's too late now. Too many men's been killed. And he's putting up his guns at the last. They'll git him 'fore many days. . . . He tol' me so.

MAYNO

You're a-lyin', gal. You know he's goin' to bring 'em down for Steve, him as was the strappingest man o' the gang. It ain't his way to be a-backing down and not pay 'em.

JANE

No, he ain't. He's a-puttin' it by, I tell you. They'll ketch him 'fore long.

MAYNO

Then what you goin' to do 'bout her in there? You cain't keep on a-foolin' her forever with your letters and money and mess from Georgy.

JANE

Well, we c'n fool 'er till she gits better, cain't we? And if she don't git better, then she'll go out happier, won't she . . . believin' Steve and Henry Berry's safe and livin' as they ought—(*She rises and goes to the cupboard*)—she so old and fearful at the door hinge skreaking even and the red rooster crowing 'fore the glim o' dawn, you know, Mayno.

(*She brings some butter and the molasses pot from the cupboard, takes the spider from the fire and puts supper on the table.*)

MAYNO

Well, go on if you will, but you cain't keep it up much longer. It'll be jes' like I said. Henry Berry'll come broozin' around some night. Sposen so?

JANE

(*Frightened*)

You reckon he'd do that. . . . No he couldn't. I tol' him about how it was with her, and besides he knows the house is watched.

MAYNO

(*Shaking her head*)

I dunno. He mought. You know the time he slipped through a whole passel o' them sher'ffs jes' to come here and git a shirt she'd made 'im? And by this time he must be a-wantin' to see her powerful bad.

JANE

(*Terrified*)

You reckon he will? No, he won't! He couldn't do that. (*Old* CUMBA *is heard calling* JANE.) Put them things in the sack with th' others, Mayno, and put 'em in the bottom, too. You c'n be fixin' her supper while I ten' to 'er. (*She goes into the rear room.* MAYNO *takes up the clothes, opens the chest at the left, pulls out a bulky burlap sack and crams the trousers, shirt and hat into it. Shutting the chest, she goes to the cupboard, takes out three plates and some knives and forks and lays them on the table. Then she begins preparing* CUMBA'S *supper on a plate.* JANE *comes to the door and speaks.*) You needn't bring her supper in here, Mayno, she's going to git up, she says. (JANE *goes back into the room.* MAYNO *shrugs her shoulders, sits down and begins to eat.* JANE *comes in supporting old* CUMBA. *She speaks to* MAYNO.) Fix her chair by the fire, Mayno.

MAYNO

(*Rising reluctantly from the table*)

Gimme time, cain't you?

(*She pulls* CUMBA'S *chair nearer to the fire.*

CUMBA *is a bent, emaciated old woman, about seventy years of age. Her face is scarred with suffering. She is a mixture of Negro and Portugese, somewhat darker than* JANE. *She is feeble and shakes with palsy.*)

CUMBA

(*Pausing, as* JANE *leads her to the fire*)

Did you say they warn't nary letter from the boys 'way out thar?

JANE

(*Looking at* MAYNO *as she settles* CUMBA *in her chair*)

No'm, there warn't no letter this time, but they'll be one soon. You see they cain't write often, not yit. They mought be ketched on account of it. 'Tain't quite time for another'n yit.

CUMBA

Mebbe so, mebbe so. But I thought they mought 'a been one. How long is it they been out thar, chile?

JANE

(*Placing the plate of food on her lap*)

Two months now, muh. And they's livin' straight and 'spectable, too. And 'twon't be long 'fore the big Governor'll pardon 'em, and they'll come back to you, and you'll be happy agin, you will that.

CUMBA

(*Brightening*)

And I'll be at the loom then, a-weavin' 'em the good shirts, won't I? And they'll be working in the fields and comin' home to a good dinner, won't they? And at night Henry Berry'll be a-playin' of his banjo like old times, won't he? (*She stops suddenly. All the brightness goes out of her face. She lets her knife fall to her plate.*) But they won't be but two of 'em, will there, Janie? Jes' two. When thar was Allen, my old man—they shot 'im over thar in the corner. (*She turns and points.*) They's a blood spot thar now. Then thar was Willie and Tom. And they ain't no tellin' how they put 'im away, chile . . . chile . . .

JANE

Now, muh, you mustn't do that!—Eat your supper. You got to git well, time Steve and Henry Berry gits back. They's allus grief with the children going, but you still got two of the boys and me.

(JANE *butters a piece of bread and hands it to her.*)

CUMBA

Mebbe so, mebbe so, chile. But . . . (*She stops.*) Whar's that letter that come from the boys last month? I wants it read agin.

JANE

But, muh, you got to eat. I'll read it after while. Let me fry you a egg.

(MAYNO *leaves the table and begins spinning at the wheel.*)

CUMBA

I ain't hongry, chile. Take them thar rations and put 'em back and read me the letter. It's enough to hear it . . . hearin' that the last of my boys is safe and ca'm and livin' once more as I'd lak 'em to.

JANE

Well, I'll git it then.

(*She goes, searches in the cupboard, and at last draws out a greasy envelope. From this she takes a sheet of paper and comes back to old* CUMBA.)

CUMBA

Read it, honey. It's the blessin' of the Lord that I's spared to learn that two o' my boys is shet of sin. But they's been a heap o' blood spilt, chile, a heap o' blood spilt . . . but they's been more tears spilt by they ol' mammy, too, and mebbe at last they'll ketch a chance to come back to her. Read it, chile.

JANE

(*Glancing at* MAYNO *and then looking at the letter*) They says they's a-gitting along well and makin' money an' . . .

CUMBA

Don't read it like that. Read what they says!

JANE

Well, I'll read it then.

(*She reads.*)

"Dear Mammy:

"We writes to let you know we're in Georgy at last, safe an' sound. We're both workin' in a store an' makin' good money. They ain't nobody knows what we done back there, an' the people is good to us. 'Twon't be long 'fore the Governor'll pardon us, and we can come back and take care o' you.

"Your lovind sons,

"Steve and Henry Berry."

CUMBA

You left out somethin', child. Don't you know they sent some money with the letter and they spoke about it.

JANE

(*Confused*)

Yes'm, that's right. I forgot it. It's on the other side, mammy. Yes'm, here it is. It says, "We're sendin' you twenty dollars to buy meat and flour with."

CUMBA

Good boys they is, they ain't never meant no harm. Willie and Tom was jes' that-a-way. Every cent they used to make a-hoein' cotton 'roun' they'd give it to they ol' mammy, an' the good Lord knows whar they's sleepin' to-night . . . but they's two spared me an' I hadn't ought to complain, I reckon. Is the money all gone, Janie?

JANE

No'm, there's some left yit, and they'll be sending more in the next letter.

(She puts the letter back into the cupboard and begins cleaning up the dishes. Old CUMBA *leans back in her chair, gazing into the fire. The hooting of an owl is heard. She stirs uneasily in her chair.* MAYNO *and* JANE *stop their work and listen. They both look at each other and then glance at old* CUMBA, *who is trembling and gripping the arms of her chair.* JANE *begins to rattle the dishes.* MAYNO *spins rapidly.)*

CUMBA

(Turning to JANE*)*

Ain't that a owl squeechin', Jane?

JANE

(Looking at MAYNO*)*

What? . . . I . . . I don't hear nothin'.

(The hooting is heard again.)

CUMBA

Ain't that it agin?

MAYNO

Aw, it's nothin' but that ol' swamp owl. He hollers 'most every night. Don't take on 'bout it.

(She shivers and stirs the fire.)

CUMBA

(Shrilly)

It sounds like some o' my boys a-makin' o' they signals down thar in the night; but 'tain't them though.

The only two that's left is a long ways off, and mebbe won't never come back.

JANE

Now, they will too.

CUMBA

'Way back yonder I loved to see 'em 'round me here, the warm fire a-burnin' and Allen thar a-working at his gear, and them that was little uns then a-playing on the floor. I didn't mind it them times. (*Her voice grows shriller.*) And now where are they? My ol' man and all the house gone from me.

MAYNO

Aw, Ma Lowrie, what's the use of all them carry-ing-ons? You reckon you're the only one that's had trouble in this world?

CUMBA

And when the rain and the wind come raring down and the cypress trees is moanin' in the dark and the owls a-honing through the night, I think on them three lyin' dead thar in the woods and the water washin' over them, and me with nothin' but their clothes to remem-ber on and show for them I was prided for.

(*Again the hooting of the owl is heard.* JANE *leaves the dishes suddenly and comes to the fire, lays more wood on, furtively wiping the tears from her eyes.* CUMBA *still looks in the fire.*)

JANE

It's time for you to lay down now.

CUMBA

(*Without noticing her*)

At times in the dark night I dream on 'em and they ain't nothin' happened and it's all like it used to be, and then I wake a-callin', and they don't answer, for they're sleepin' out naked in the cold.

MAYNO

(*Shrugging her shoulders*)

Jes' listen at her!—Ma Lowrie, cain't you be quiet a bit? (*Lowering her voice.*) Lord, you're as techous as a' old hen!

JANE

(*Half sobbing*)

What makes you carry on like that? It cain't do no good. Ain't Henry Berry tol' you a hundred times that he's buried all three of 'em down thar in the swamp. And he's skeered to tell the place for fear them sher'ffs'll dig 'em up and git the money for 'em. Don't take on so. They's put away with praying, and you'd better lie down now.

(*She looks at* MAYNO.)

CUMBA

Yes, they mought be buried in the swamp down thar, and when it rains the river rises and washes over 'em, them that used to pull at my dress when I was at the wash— But Old Master sends the sun and the rain, and the Book says we ought to be satisfied. (*The owl's hoot is heard again.* CUMBA *looks at the door and shivers.*) Help me in now, chile. I didn't mean to say all that, but I'm done. An' ol' woman's heart is a foolish thing . . . a foolish thing. . . .

(JANE *helps her into the room at the left. A moment later she reappears. She looks at* MAYNO *inquisitively.*)

MAYNO

Sounded like Henry Berry's hootin', didn't it?

JANE

Yes, I'm afraid it's him, after all I tol' him. Oh, what makes him do it? But it's like I said. He's givin' in now, he's quittin' at the last. And he's set on seein' her once more or it's some of his quair notions, somethin' he's wropped up in gittin'.

(*Three knocks are heard at the door.* JANE *runs and lifts the heavy bar, and* HENRY BERRY LOWRIE *walks in.*)

MAYNO

Henry Berry!

(*He starts to speak but* JANE *lays her finger on her lips and leads him towards the fire. He takes off his hat and bows wearily to* MAYNO.

He is a man of handsome personal appearance. The color of his skin is a mixed white and yellowish brown, almost copper-colored. Just below his left eye is a crescent-shaped scar. Despite the look of weariness, his countenance is expressive in a high degree of firmness and courage. His forehead is broad and high, his eyes large and keen, his hair thick and inclined to curl. He wears a black beard. From appearances he is about twenty-six years of age, a little above medium height, well-knit, broad-shouldered, and well-proportioned throughout. He wears a broad, black felt hat, brown corduroy coat, dark woolen trousers, and calf-skin boots. In a belt around his waist he carries two pistols. From this belt a strap passes upward and supports a repeating rifle behind. He also carries a long-bladed knife stuck in his belt. He takes a seat at the fire, putting his rifle in the corner, but retaining his other arms. JANE *runs to the door at the rear and makes sure that it is closed tight. Then she hurries to* HENRY BERRY.

JANE

Brother, what made you do it! The house is watched an' . . .

HENRY BERRY

I know it, Sis, but I had to come. I'm quittin' . . . to-night. Is she asleep?

(*He jerks his head towards the room at the left.*)

JANE

No, I've jes' helped her in. That's the reason we couldn't make no sign with the light.

HENRY BERRY

I couldn't figure what the trouble was. I hooted 'til my head hurt. But I was goin' to risk it anyhow.

JANE

What'll she think if she sees you! Oh, hurry and go away!

HENRY BERRY

Naw, I got to see her. After to-night 'twon't matter. Bring me a bite to eat, Sis. How is she?

MAYNO

I reckon she's on the mend. . . .

JANE

(*Frightened*)

Will they git you to-night? What do you mean by sich talk?

HENRY BERRY

Never mind. They'll git me . . . when I'm dead, all right, no doubt o' that. I'm taking the gear off at last. The ol' man's gone, Willie and Tom's gone, and they got Steve last week, and I'm the last o' the gang. I'm tired, damned tired of it all, Sis.

JANE

But I tell you, you cain't give up like that. You got to keep on fightin' till you git a chance to git away!

HENRY BERRY

Naw, it's too late now. If they'd 'a let me, I'd 'a

lived straight, but after the first trouble I had to keep killin' to live. Well, I'm done killin', now . . . 'cept one man, and they ain't no use of you knowin' who it is. You'll know soon enough. One man can't stand it allus, and they'll scrush him at the last.

(JANE *sits in her chair weeping softly.* HENRY BERRY *lays his hand gently on her head. Trying to appear cheerful, he turns to* MAYNO.)

Mayno, bring me a bite to eat.

(*He sits at the table, facing the front.* MAYNO *gets a plate of food and puts it before him. He eats hungrily.*)

MAYNO

Whar'd they put 'im, Henry Berry?

HENRY BERRY

I ain't been able to find out, Mayno. Piled him in some of their rotten graveyards, I reckon, when he loved to run the woods with th' other wild things like him.

MAYNO

What'd they do with his money?

HENRY BERRY

I dunno. Got that, too, I reckon. But you needn't to worry. Jane! (JANE *looks up.*) Here, I've fixed for you-all. Here's money enough to last you three after I'm gone.

(*He stops eating and pulls a bag of money out of his pocket.*)

JANE

But, brother . . .

HENRY BERRY

Never mind, take it and take care o' her. It's the last thing I c'n do for her and you.

JANE

But she won't use it, knowin' how you come by it.

HENRY BERRY

She won't?

JANE

No, she won't. She'll starve first, and you know it. You know all them fixin's you sent her. She give 'em all away, the stove and the stool with three legs and everything. And when she thought you and Steve was livin' straight in Georgy, she give away that gold chain you brung her. She's feared you hadn't got it honest.

HENRY BERRY

(*Softly*)

Yes, yes, she's allus been too good fer us. (*He leaves the table and takes a seat near the fire.*) Still that chain was bought honest. . . . But you three's got to live, ain't ye? Take that money, and don't tell 'er. (JANE *puts the money in the chest.*) Mayno, is my ol' banjo still here?

MAYNO

Yeah, in thar.

HENRY BERRY

I been wantin' to knock her a little for a long time. And I want to knock her a little the las' night.

JANE

The las' night! It ain't the las' night! If you'd go now you'd git away. Why do you talk like that?

(She is interrupted by a loud cry. Old CUMBA *stands in the door at the rear.)*

CUMBA

It's you, it's you, Henry Berry! Come back from Georgy. I knowed you'd come. I knowed. . . . *(She totters to* HENRY BERRY *and throws her arms around him. He kisses her on the forehead. Her look is one of unmingled joy. Suddenly the hurt look comes back into her face.)* Why you come back a-wearin' of your guns?

HENRY BERRY

(Helping her to the fire)

I'm just wearin' 'em. I didn't want to be ketched empty. I'm leavin' in a few minutes and le's us enjoy ourselves, and forgit about Georgy.

CUMBA

No, they's somethin' wrong. Whar's Steve?

HENRY BERRY

(Looking at MAYNO *and* JANE*)*

He's waitin' for me . . . out thar.

(He points toward the swamp.)

CUMBA

Why didn't he come in wid you? Is he well and strong? How I'd love to see 'im!

HENRY BERRY

One of us had to wait for th' othern, and he's all right. How you feelin', mammy? Is your haid better now?

CUMBA

Yes, I'm gittin' better now. I wants to git well time you and Steve comes home for good. (*Stroking his hand.*) Has the Gov'nor pardoned ye already?

HENRY BERRY

No, mammy, not jest yit. But it'll be all right soon. . . . Steve and me's jest passin' through. . . . Now le's us enjoy ourselves. I got to be movin' in a minute. Steve's waiting for me. . . . Mebbe we'll talk about Georgy some other time. . . . Mayno, bring me my ol' music box.

CUMBA

Yes, yes, git it and let 'im play for me.

(MAYNO *brings the banjo from the next room.* HENRY BERRY *tunes it.* CUMBA *sits gazing in the fire, a troubled look on her face.*)

HENRY BERRY

You want me to play 'bout Job's Coffin hanging in the sky? (*Strangely.*) That was Steve's piece.

JANE
(*Nervously*)
Don't, don't play that. It's too lonesome.
(*She shivers.*)

HENRY BERRY
What piece you want me to play?
(*To* CUMBA. *She makes no reply.* HENRY BERRY *looks at her. He strums several bars, his face gradually losing its tense expression.*)
What you want me to play, muh?

CUMBA
Play anything. Some o' the ol' pieces.

HENRY BERRY
I'll play that piece 'bout poor John Hardy.
(*He plays and sings three stanzas of the ballad "John Hardy."*)

John Hard - y was a mean and—
dis - per - a - ted man, He

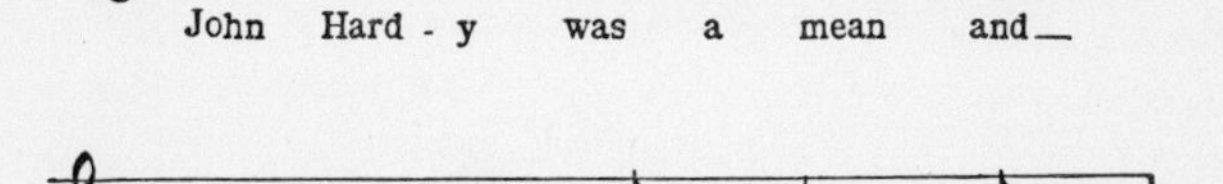

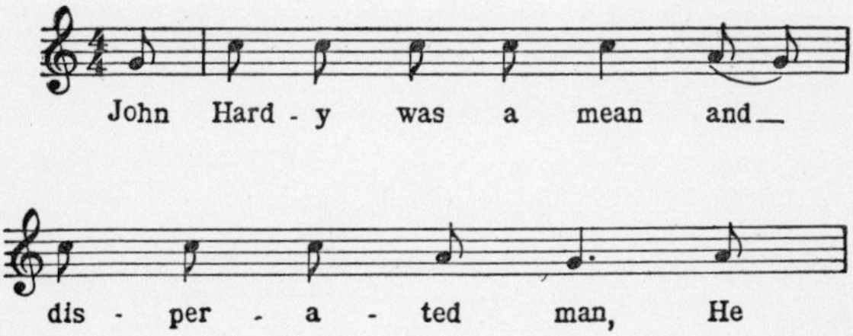

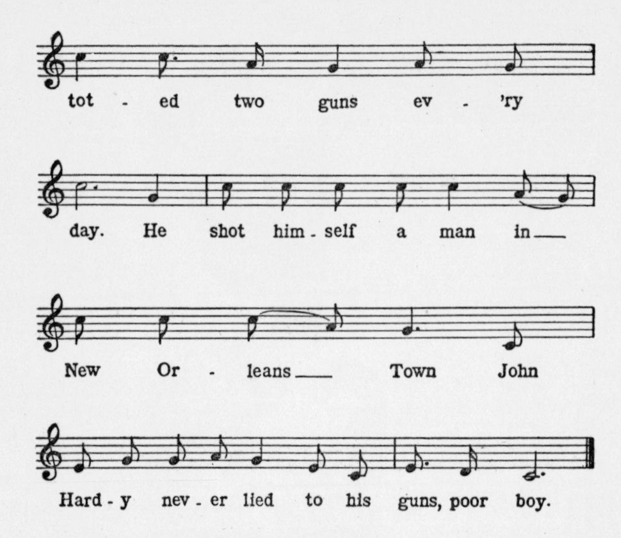

He's been to the east and he's been to the west
And he's been this wide world round,
He's been to the river an' been baptized,
An' he's been on his hanging ground, poor boy.

John Hardy's father was standing by,
Saying, "Johnnie, what have you done?"
He murdered a man in the same ol' town,
You ought a-seed him a-using of his guns, poor boy.
(*He stops and gazes pensively before him.*)

CUMBA

(*Looking anxiously at* HENRY BERRY)

What's the matter, son? You don't play it like you used to.

Scene from *The Last of the Lowries,* a play of the Robeson County Outlaws, by Paul Greene. MAYNO, Henry Berry's sister-in-law (Rachel Freeman); HENRY BERRY LOWRIE (Ernest Neiman); CUMBA, his mother (Elizabeth Taylor); JANE, his sister (Ruth Penny).

CUMBA: What's the matter, son? You don't play it like you used to.

HENRY BERRY

It ain't nothing. I'll play yo' other piece now, that Florelly song.

CUMBA

Yes, play it. Allen allus said 'twas a good piece.

HENRY BERRY

The Fair Florella
An Old Ballad

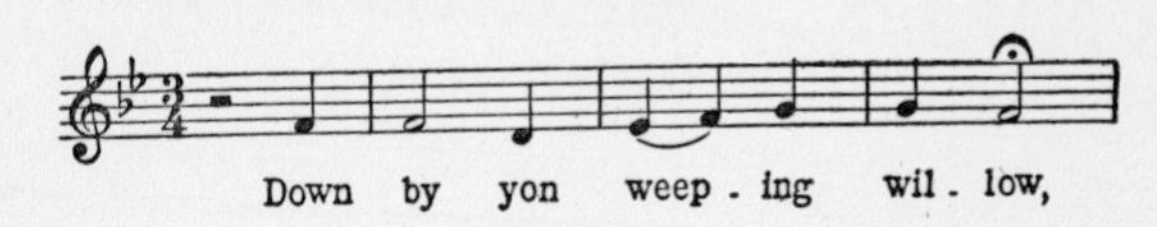

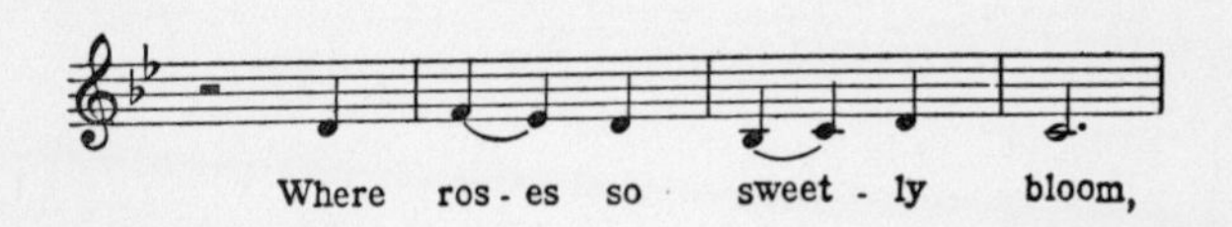

She died not broken hearted,
No sickness her befell,
But in one moment parted
From all she loved so well.

Down on her knees before him,
She begged 'im for her life,
But deep into her bosom
He plunged the fatal knife.

(*Before the last verse ends, owl hoots are heard outside.* HENRY BERRY *stops, listening. The banjo slips through his hands to the floor. All three look at him questioningly.*)

CUMBA

What is it, boy? Don't look that-a-way.

(*Again the hooting of an owl is heard.* HENRY BERRY *rises to his feet, takes his rifle from the chimney corner and stands an instant tensely silent. Slowly his defensive attitude changes to one of despair. They watch him anxiously as he comes back to his former place in the room, looks down at his banjo, makes a move as if to pick it up, then turns to* CUMBA.)

HENRY BERRY

Well, I'm goin'. I've sorto' tried to be a fitten boy to you, but I reckon I made poor outs at it.

(*He bends and kisses her. She rises and clings to him.*)

CUMBA

You ain't a-goin' air ye? It'll be for the las' time and I know it.

HENRY BERRY

Yes'm, I got to go. Didn't you hear Steve's signal? He's a-waitin'.

(*Making an indefinite motion with his hand toward the swamp, he loosens her hold, kisses* JANE *and makes a sign for* MAYNO *to follow him. They both go out.* CUMBA *wrings her hands and follows him toward the door. Then she becomes calm.*)

CUMBA

Let him go off now, an' I'll never see 'im agin. His sperit's broke and he won't be a-goin' back to Georgy. I see it in his face that he's quittin' it all.

JANE

No'm he ain't, he's a-goin' straight back. . . . He and Steve is.

CUMBA

No, he ain't a-goin' back. Cain't I see what's in his face? They'll git 'im and 'twon't be long, and then Steve'll be shot down next, and there'll be only a handful o' their clothes for me to look at. (JANE *weeps silently.*) Whar's Mayno?

JANE

She's jes' stepped out a minute. She'll be back.

CUMBA

Yes, and I know, they're goin' to git 'im. They's a-setting for him thar in the black night.

JANE

No'm, they ain't, I tell you. They'll never git Henry Berry. (OLD CUMBA *shakes her head mumbling. She goes to the chest at the left and takes out the burlap bag. The lid of the chest falls.* JANE *starts up.*) Put it back, put it back. You mustn't look at 'em to-night. Come back to the fire.

(*She tries to take the bag from her.*)

CUMBA

No, chil', I ain't. I'm goin' to look at all that's left of 'em.

JANE

Let 'em be!

CUMBA

(*Waving her off*)

No, git away. Soon Henry Berry's 'll be in there, too. (*She stops and looks at the bag.*) Janie, who's been foolin' wi' this? What's . . .

(*She hurries to the table and holding the sack close to the candle, opens it. She catches hold of a coat sleeve and draws out Steve's coat. A gasping dry sound comes from her throat. She drops the bag and holds the coat in her trembling hands.*)

It's Steve's! How come it here? It's Steve's!—one I made 'im myself.

JANE

Oh, muh, let . . . What ails you?

CUMBA

I s'picioned it! And they been foolin' me.

JANE

(*Hopelessly*)

Yes'm, it's Steve's.

(CUMBA *sways to and fro.*)

CUMBA

You been foolin' me! You been foolin' me! (*She stands rigid for a moment, then speaks in a hard, lifeless voice.*) It warn't right to fool me like that. . . . When'd it happen?

JANE

Las' week. . . . They got 'im down on the big road by the swamp, an' . . .

CUMBA

Hush! Don't tell me 'bout it. I'm afflicted and defeated enough now. They's only one left and they'll git 'im soon. . . . Did they put Steve away like a man?

JANE

I dunno. The sheriff give 'is clothes to me.

(*A shot is heard in the distance, followed by a woman's scream.*)

CUMBA

(*Starting up and speaking in a shrill voice*)

They got 'im now! They got 'im now! The last un's gone!

(*She tries to go out at the door.* JANE *stops her.*)

JANE

(*Catching her by the arm*)

Don't do that!

(CUMBA *goes back to the sack, picks up* STEVE'S *coat and stares at it dully.*)

CUMBA

They tuck 'em all now. They tuck 'em all.

JANE

Muh, it had to come. An' it's better that-a-way.

CUMBA

(*Dully*)

Better that-a-way?

JANE

Yes, it's better like that. They was wrong from the jump.

CUMBA

Wrong! My boys was good boys. They ain't never . . . (*Raising her hands above her head, she speaks fiercely.*) May Ol' Master send his fires on them that done it! An' . . .

JANE

(*Sobbing*)

Oh, why'd they do it!

CUMBA

No. It says as how we'd ought to love 'em 'at does us wrong.

(*She closes her eyes, swaying slightly from side to side.*)

JANE

Let me help you to lie down now!

CUMBA

Yes, it's better that-a-way, I reckon. (*Her face shows resignation to sorrow. She speaks with a sort of joy in her voice.*) An' I won't be livin' in hope and fear no mo', will I? (*Slowly.*) And when the owls hoot through the swamp at night, and the whippoorwills sing in the thicket at dark, I won't have cause to think that's one o' my own a-givin' of 'is signals, an' tryin' to slip back to 'is ol' home, the only place he loves, —will I? (*She drops down into the chair behind the table.*) An' I won't lie awake at night, thinkin' they're in danger . . . for He's done give 'em His peace at last.

(MAYNO *enters running. Old* CUMBA *stands up.*)

MAYNO

He shot 'isself. He shot 'isself! He give me this coat to give to you, an' then the sheriffs crope from the thicket at 'im, but he shot 'isself 'fore they got to 'im, and they tuck 'im and toted 'im off!

(*She drops into her chair exhausted, rocking to and fro. Old* CUMBA *takes the coat from her, looks at it, and then puts it in the sack. She puts* STEVE'S *coat in also and stands looking down at the bag.*)

CUMBA

Thar's all that's left o' them I loved . . . a bundle o' clothes to show for my man an' four grown sons. (*She stops an instant.*) And you'll all sleep quiet at the last. (*She stands a moment silent, then shrilly.*) But they're all gone, and what call hev I got to be living more. . . .

(*She raises her hand as if in a curse. But her face softens, and as the curtain falls, she stands with both hands outstretched on the clothes, blessing them.*)

[1] It is interesting to note that the actual story (see Introduction page xxviii) of the old Lowrie mother somewhat parallels that of Maurya in Synge's *Riders to the Sea.* In the one case the mother sees her sons sacrificed before the power of the law. In the other she sees them claimed by the terribleness of the sea. So far as the suffering is concerned, the forces in both cases might be the same.

APPENDIX

THE LANGUAGE OF THE PLAYS

Observations on the Pronunciation of the Dialects of North Carolina

With a few obvious exceptions, the personages depicted in the dramas here printed speak one or another of the dialects used by the uncultured whites and negroes of North Carolina. In connection with this effort to utilize for dramatic purposes the folk speech of a relatively small district of the South, several facts should be borne in mind. In the first place, it is an error to assume, as appears to be done frequently outside the South, that all Southern whites speak practically alike and that the difference between their speech and that of Southern negroes is insignificant. Although, it is true, certain peculiarities of pronunciation and certain turns of phrase are more or less common to all speakers of English in the South Atlantic States, considerable differences both in vocabulary and in pronunciation are discernible between numerous districts of this section, in some instances even when these districts adjoin each other. The dialect spoken by the native whites of eastern North Carolina, for example, is markedly different from that of the Carolina highlands, and among the Blue Ridge and Alleghany mountains clear variations in language may sometimes be noted as one passes from valley to valley or from "cove" to "cove." Again, although it is true that the English-speaking negroes of the South, having borrowed their language from the whites, have much in common with them and have even exerted an appreciable influence upon the speech of their white neighbors, yet no Southerner would confuse the dialect of a typical uneducated Carolina negro with that of even the most backward Carolina white. Moreover, in North Carolina, as elsewhere, dialect varies from family to family and from individual to individual, and even the same person changes his speech to suit his humor, his company, or other occasional circumstances. What Horace Kephart says of the Carolina mountaineer is true of the uncultured throughout the State. "The same man," writes the author of *Our Southern Highlanders,* "at different times may say *can't* and *cain't, set* and *sot, jest* and *jes'* and *jist, atter* and *arter, seed* and *seen, here* and *hyur* and *hyar, heerd* and *heern* and *heard, took* and *tuk*." These facts, obvious as they are to the Southerner, need to be emphasized if this volume is to be read intelligently outside the South.

It should also be observed that the dialects of North Carolina, like those of other districts, cannot be correctly represented by any conventional system of printed signs. As Professor Sheldon has pointed out, "the written [language] . . . is, speaking, generally, only a later and inexact representation for the eye of the language as spoken, that is, of the real language," and, with an alphabet so imperfect as ours, it is clearly impossible to depict accurately even the more obvious peculiarities of Southern pronunciation, to say nothing of the subtler differences between the various speech-islands of the South. Few of the differences between North Carolinese and standard American English are capable of exact representation by ordinary letters; most of them are so elusive as to escape even the most elaborate system of phonetic symbols. In the words of a distinguished authority on the history of English speech, "You could not denote [such variations in language] if you would and if you could, you would be encumbered, rather than aided, by the multiplicity of signs." Or, to adopt the language of a queer old eighteenth century spelling reformer, "delicate ears alone can discern what only delicate organs can convey."

In view of these difficulties, it became necessary to adopt an arbitrary standard of spelling for the dialects represented in this volume. In establishing this norm the editors have been guided by several considerations. To begin with, as may be observed in the work of Synge and other serious writers of dialect literature, successful dialect writing depends rather upon picturesqueness of vocabulary and idiom than upon spelling. In the best dialect literature spelling is of purely incidental value. Again, in the case of many words and phrases the difference between North Carolinese and American English as spoken by all except the most careful speakers outside the South, is too slight to justify any change in the accepted spelling. On the other hand, the combined labors of Southern dialect writers for nearly a century have established for certain words and phrases a conventional standard which has come to be associated in the public mind with any effort to represent on paper the speech of the typical Southerner. In considering the matter of traditional dialect spelling, a distinction should, however, be made between legitimate variations from standard practice and those spellings which are of no assistance in pronunciation and are merely "bad." Josh Billings, it is recorded, began his career as a humorist by changing his famous "Essa on the Muel" from ordinary to "phonetic" spelling, but most of Josh Billings' spellings, however funny they may have been to our fathers, have little justification phonetically. The same is true of much of the spelling used by Artemus Ward, Petroleum V. Nasby, Sut Lovingood, and other humorous writers who have helped to establish the tradition of dialect spelling in America. For many words contained in the dramas here printed, new spellings could be devised which, regarded phonetically, would perhaps represent the actual Carolina pronunciation more accurately than either the standard or the traditional orthography; yet any such gain in accuracy would in most cases be more than offset by a resulting loss in intelligibility. In view of these facts and of the alarm with which spelling reforms are liable to be regarded by the average reader, it has been deemed advisable to depart from standard usage only in those cases where traditional practice in Southern dialect literature clearly points the way or where the use of "phonetic" spelling runs no risk of irritating or distracting the reader.

Although nothing short of an intimate acquaintance

with spoken North Carolinese can insure an absolutely correct pronunciation of the written language, the following observations may be of assistance to readers who know the dialects of the South chiefly through the medium of the printed page. Owing to limitations of space, only the more general and characteristic peculiarities of the Carolina dialects can be considered here. A more detailed discussion is now in preparation and will, it is hoped, appear ere long in *Studies in Philology,* published by the University of North Carolina.

As regards consonantal sounds, the spelling adopted in this volume requires little comment. In general the consonants, except *r,* may be understood to have the same value as in standard American English. For practical purposes it may be assumed that *r* is omitted by native Carolinians whenever it stands before other consonants or is final. The result is usually a slight change in the quality or length of the preceding vowel. Thus *floor* and *tore* are practically indistinguishable in pronunciation from *flow* and *toe,* and the Carolina pronunciation of *corn* rhymes with the standard pronunciation of *dawn.* There is also a strong tendency to omit the *r*-sound between vowels (as in *be'yin'* for *burying* [a funeral] and *ve'y* for *very*), and even in some cases when it stands after a consonant and before a vowel (as in *hund'ed* for *hundred* and *p'oduce* for *produce*). In order to avoid undue distortion in the form of the words, *r* is generally retained in the spelling here used except in forms such as *cuss* for *curse, fust* for *first,* and *nuss* for *nurse,* where the meaning is easily identified and the spelling is clearly justified by tradition. The combination *er* is also freely used, especially in final position, to represent the indistinct sound heard in the Carolina pronunciation of such words as *tobacco* but lacking in more exact speech.

As appears from the examination of a large body of dialect literature, the practice of spelling together groups of words pronounced as a unit is frequently open to objection; hence it has been followed here only in a few well established cases such as *gimme* for *give me, mebbe* for *maybe,* and *nemmine* for *never mind.* The highly characteristic Southern pronunciation of *you all* (practically *yawl*) is indicated merely by a hyphen (*you-all*).

Of the many phonetic differences between the dialects of North Carolina and standard American or English usage, several require special attention.

For the short *o* sound heard in the standard English pronunciation of *cob, dog, fog, frog, God, gone, gospel, hog,* and similar words, the typical uncultured North Carolinian generally substitutes a sound closely approximating that of the vowel in *law.* Or, to put it another way, in North Carolina *God* rhymes with *sawed,* and *hog* is pronounced as though it were spelled *hawg.*

The dialects of North Carolina show few traces of the so-called "broad *a*" and none at all of the middle or Continental *a* recommended by the dictionaries for such words as *branch, can't, France,* and *grass.* Except before *r* the sound in such cases is usually that of *a* in *lamb,* sometimes slightly drawled. The same vowel is heard in the Carolina pronunciation of *ant, aunt, bath, calf, dance, gape, half,* and similar words. Thus, in eastern North Carolina, *calm, palm,* and *psalm* rhyme with *dam.* When the *a* sound (written *a* or *ea*) precedes *r,* the *r* practically disappears and the vowel approaches the sound of *aw* in *law* so closely as to be easily distinguishable from the New England pronunciation of *a* in the same position. Thus, in North Carolina *yard,* though not quite a perfect rhyme for *sawed,* is much more nearly so than it is for *hard* as pronounced by the New Englander. (Cf. *Dialect Notes,* I, 34.) As elsewhere in the South Atlantic States, the "broad *a*" is most frequently heard in the eastern Carolina pronunciation of *ask, ma, master, pa!* A characteristic though not exclusively Carolina pronunciation is *cain't* (cf. *ain't*) for *can't.* In *calf, can't, car, carpet, Carter, garden,* (*re*)*guard*(*s*), and other words in which the accented *a* is preceded by a *c* or *g*(*u*), the glide-sound following the consonant and popularly supposed to be an earmark of aristocracy in eastern Virginia and North Carolina, is seldom heard except among negroes and whites of the older generation.

In the North Carolina pronunciation of *apple, ash, bag, candle, cash, have, rabbit, saddle, spasm,* and similar words, the accented vowel is generally somewhat flattened and is occasionally drawled. Important exceptions are *ketch* for *catch, chomp* for *champ, flop* for *flap, stomp* for *stamp, strop* for *strap, tossel* for *tassel,* and *tromp*(*le*) for *tramp*(*le*). A similar substitution is frequently heard in the pronunciation of *barrel, barrow, narrow, spargus* (asparagus), and *sparrow.*

The short *e* sound heard in the standard pronunciation of *any, bed, bury, dead, friend, heifer, Reynolds, said, says,* and similar words is not uniformly preserved in the dialects of North Carolina. A frequent and characteristic substitute is short *i,* especially as in Anglo-Irish, before *m* or *n.* Thus *end* becomes *ind; Evans, Ivans* or *Ivins; fence, fince; Jenny, Jinny; men, min; pen, pin; yesterday, yistidy.* Short *i* is also the accepted vowel in the Carolina pronunciation of *again, get, kettle, project, ten,* and *yet.* Again, among negroes and uneducated whites the accented vowel of *dead, edge, leg, neck,* and *sedge* is frequently replaced by the sound of *a* in *age. Keg, wrestle, yellow, yes,* and a few other words occasionally have the same accented vowel as *rag,* and in the more remote districts *deaf* rhymes with *leaf.*

Among negroes and certain rustics *bear, declare, fair, stair, pair, swear, their, there,* and similar words requently have the same accented vowel as *bar* and *star,* but *care, scare,* and *scarce* are pronounced as though spelled *keer, skeer,* and *skeerce.* In the pronunciation of negroes *scarce* rhymes with *face.*

The obscure vowel sound heard in the standard pronunciation of the unaccented syllables of such words as *ago, children, China, cupboard, famous, liquor, mother,* and *nation* is not only preserved in the Carolina pronunciation of these and similar words, but is often substituted where in more precise enunciation other vowels are required. Its extensive occurrence is one of the chief indications of the "laziness" frequently charged against Southern speakers generally. Because of the practical impossibility of representing with ordinary letters the more difficult examples of slurring in the dialects of North Carolina without deforming the words beyond recognition, the standard spelling is preserved except in a few cases where tradition justifies the substitution of *o, a,* or *er.*

For the short *e* sound heard in the standard pronunciation of *certain, learn, search, serve,* and similar words, mountaineers and negroes are likely to substitute the *a* sound of *Clark. Heard* is frequently pronounced *hyeard. Girl* may become *gall;* the pronunciation *gyerl* is confined to a few older whites and negroes.

In *been, breeches, sleek, teat,* and a few other words, the accented vowel of standard pronunciation is uniformly replaced by that of *bit. Creature* is pronounced *creeter* or *critter.*

For the accented short *i* heard in the standard pronunciation of such words as *bring, dinner, hinder, linen, miracle, pith, pin, since, spirit, thin, thing, think,* the uneducated Carolinian is likely to substitute a short *e* sound. That is to say, in the mouth of the typical uncultured speaker the accented vowel of *pith* and *hinder* is that heard in the standard pronunciation of *death* and *tender.* Other noteworthy departures from standard pronunciation are *genuaine* for *genuine, favoraite* for *favorite, highstrikes* for *hysterics, reptaile* for *reptile, eetch* for *itch,* and *mischeevous* for *mischievous.* In North Carolinese the universal pronunciation of *Mrs.* is merely *Miz,* with the final consonant somewhat prolonged. (Cf. Krapp, *The Pronunciation of Stand-*

ard English in America, New York, 1919, p. 122.)

For the accented vowel of *boar, bore, door, floor, force, gourd, porch, pork,* and most other words of the same class, the native Carolinian substitutes a long *o*. The *r* is of course lost. Thus, in typical North Carolinese of the remote rural districts *boar, door, floor,* and *sore* are homonymous respectively with *beau, dough, flow,* and *sew*. Noteworthy also are the pronunciations *janders* for *jaundice, sassy* for *saucy,* and *faward* for *forward*.

The *u* sound heard in the standard English pronunciation of *lose* requires special consideration. As in certain sections of America outside North Carolina, *food, proof, roof, root, soon, spoon,* and certain other words have the sound of *oo* heard in *balloon,* whereas *butcher, broom, coop, Cooper, hoof, hoop, Hooper,* and *room* have a short *u* sound like that heard in the standard pronunciation of *bush*. Again, in the Carolina pronunciation of *cute, dew, due, duty, stew, tune,* and *Tuesday,* the accented vowel is preceded by a glide sound as though the words in question were spelled *cyute,* etc.; in *absolute(ly), blue, deuce, glue, Lucy, Luke, rude, Sue, true,* and most other words of this class the glide is never present. In North Carolina, as elsewhere in the South, the "correct" differentiation in this matter is one of the best criteria of native speech. No North Carolinian of uncontaminated linguistic habits would, for example, pronounce "New tunes are due to Sue," *Noo toons are doo to Syue*.

A noteworthy departure from the accented vowel heard in the standard pronunciation of such words as *pull, woman, wood,* are *put, took,* and *soot,* which among older speakers generally rhyme respectively with *gut, tuck,* and *smut.*

For the so-called "long *i*" of standard usage the Carolina lowlander frequently substitutes a sound composed of the *u* of *but* followed by the vowel of *tea.* In a number of words—notably *advice, (al)might(y), bite, cipher, (de)light, disciple, ice, like, mice, nice, night, right(eous), title, trifle,* and *twice*—the latter is the accepted pronunciation along the coast as in other parts of the South Atlantic seaboard, and its "correct" usage is one of the best linguistic earmarks of the native Southerner. In the matter of "long *i*" the Carolina mountaineer is much closer than the lowlander to the ordinary pronunciation in the North and the Middle West.

Analogous to the treatment of "long *i*" is that of the *ou* sound heard in the standard pronunciation of *couch* and *town.* Most words containing this sound are pronounced much as they are outside the South, but in certain cases—notably *doubt, house, louse, mouse, mouth,* and *south*—the first element of the diphthong is replaced by the vowel of *met.* Less frequently the same combination of short *e* and *u* is heard in *cow, cloud, down, flour, flower, found, foul, fowl, how, howl, now, plough,* and *sow* (a female hog). The ability to use this sound "correctly" is another excellent test of Southern speech. Among the mountains the *au* sound appears to be the rule. Except in the most remote districts the diphthong lacks the flat, nasal, drawl adopted by many Northerners who attempt to imitate Southern dialect.

For the *oi* sound heard in the standard pronunciation

of such words as *anoint, hoist, join(t), joist, point, poison, spoil,* and *tenderloin,* negroes, mountaineers, and other ultra-conservative speakers substitute "long *i.*"

TOM PEETE CROSS.

The University of Chicago.